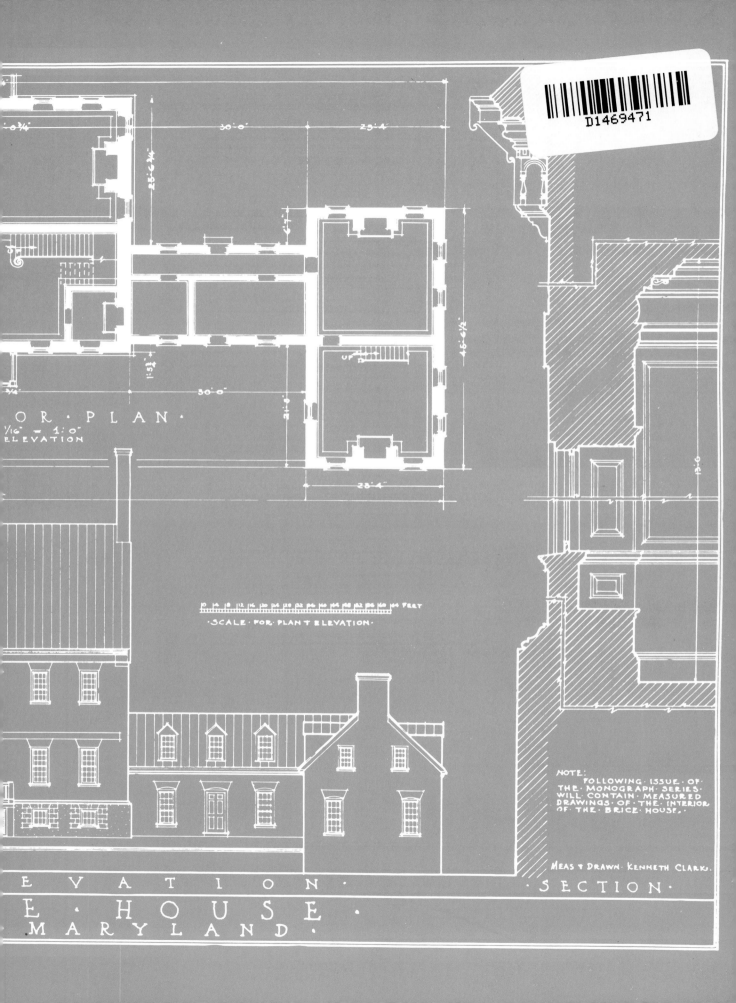

EARLY AMERICAN SOUTHERN HOMES

Other National Historical Society Publications:

THE IMAGE OF WAR: 1861–1865

TOUCHED BY FIRE: A PHOTOGRAPHIC PORTRAIT OF THE CIVIL WAR

WAR OF THE REBELLION: OFFICIAL RECORDS
  OF THE UNION AND CONFEDERATE ARMIES

OFFICIAL RECORDS OF THE UNION AND CONFEDERATE NAVIES
  IN THE WAR OF THE REBELLION

HISTORICAL TIMES ILLUSTRATED ENCYCLOPEDIA OF THE CIVIL WAR

A TRAVELLER'S GUIDE TO GREAT BRITAIN SERIES

For information about National Historical Society Publications, write:
Historical Times, Inc., 2245 Kohn Road, Box 8200, Harrisburg, Pennsylvania 17105

Architectural Treasures of Early America

EARLY AMERICAN SOUTHERN HOMES

From material originally published as
The White Pine Series of Architectural Monographs
edited by
Russell F. Whitehead and Frank Chouteau Brown

Lisa C. Mullins, Editor

Roy Underhill, Consultant

A Publication of
THE NATIONAL HISTORICAL SOCIETY

Copyright © 1987 by the National Historical Society

All rights reserved. Printed in the United States of America. No part of this book may be used or reproduced in any manner whatsoever without written permission except in the case of brief quotations embodied in critical articles and reviews.

Library of Congress Cataloging-in-Publication Data

Early American southern homes.
    (Architectural treasures of early America; 8)
      1. Architecture—Southern States. 2. Architecture, Georgian—Southern States. 3. Mansions—Southern States.
I. Mullins, Lisa C. II. Underhill, Roy. III. Series:
Architectural treasures of Early America (Harrisburg, Pa.); 8.
NA720.E15   1988   728.8'3'0975   87-14203
ISBN 0-918678-27-7

The original photographs reproduced in this publication are from the collection of drawings and photographs in "The White Pine Monograph Series, Collected and Edited by Russell F. Whitehead, The George P. Lindsay Collection." The collection, part of the research and reference collections of The American Institute of Architects, Washington, D.C., was acquired by the Institute in 1955 from the Whitehead estate, through the cooperation of Mrs. Russell F. Whitehead, and the generosity of the Weyerhauser Timber Company, which purchased the collection for presentation to the Institute. The research and reference collections of the Institute are available for public use. A written request for such use is required so that space may be reserved and assistance made available.

PROPERTY OF THE
LIBRARY OF THE CHATHAMS
CHATHAM, NJ 07928

CONTENTS

AN "UNKNOWN YOUNG MAN"

In 1925 a portrait of an "unknown young man painted by C. W. Peale" went on the auction block. The anonymous subject of the painting looked vibrantly and confidently from the canvas. On the table beside him lay drawing instruments and the plan of a house. Behind him stood a classical portico and scaffolding. No one knew at the time that this "unknown young man" was responsible for the most beautiful homes ever built in America. No one knew William Buckland.

William Buckland's story emerged slowly in this century. In the original 1929 monograph on the Hammond-Harwood House of Annapolis (Chapter 3) he was mistakenly identified as *Matthew* Buckland from Philadelphia. His work at Gunston Hall (Chapter 6) was attributed to "convict craftsmen from England" and to the "importation of the finished product from England." Now, scholars have pieced together his career as a master craftsman of the colonial Chesapeake. Architectural historians have identified the work of the individual carvers in his employ, and are gradually retrieving his creations from the insults of the centuries.

George Mason, the "Father of the Bill of Rights," brought William Buckland to America in 1755. As was the custom of his class, Mason followed the advice of William Fitzhugh to "get a Carpenter, & Bricklayer Servants, & send them in here to serve 4 or 5 years, in which time of their service, they might reasonably build a substantial good house." He began the simple brick exterior of Gunston Hall overlooking the Potomac, while his younger brother, Thomson Mason, who was studying law in London, sought out a suitable joiner and carver. Thomson found Buckland; twenty-one years old, having just completed his apprenticeship. Thomson engaged him as an indentured servant to serve four years in America.

The young Buckland was eager to show his skill. Gunston Hall soon became a catalogue of the latest London styles. William Buckland had learned his trade as an apprentice to his uncle; a London woodcarver, joiner, and publisher of architectural books. Buckland had fifteen of these books when he died. The Gunston Hall dining room in the Chinese style was derived from one of them, Chippendale's *Gentleman and Cabinetmaker's Director*. This room is the first known chinoiserie in colonial America. The double ring fretwork over the doors in the "Palladian room" echos that shown in Batty Langley's *City and Country Builder's and Workman's Treasury of Designs*. The southern garden porch was inspired by another Langley book, *Gothic Architecture* and is the first expression of the Gothic Revival in America. These were not only firsts, they were magnificent.

But time takes its toll. A servant's stairs, probably built at the suggestion of Buckland, was removed. Mouldings were taken from the fireplace to use on doorways. Alterations were made throughout the years, including the 1950 restoration by Fiske Kimball.

Architectural detectives began exploring at Gunston Hall in 1982. Charles Phillips and Paul Buchanan traced wear patterns, exposed ghostly paint ridges, and probed countless nail holes. They found that the house was much more elaborately ornamented than anyone had imagined. Decorative carvings had been everywhere, even on the window muntins. The entrance hall originally had twelve more pilasters, an elaborate frieze, and a false door. These have now been replaced, and work is underway on the other rooms. Slowly the house is returning to Buckland.

Buckland finished his indenture to Mason in 1759. Although technically a servant, he was highly respected and treated more like a member of the family. He left with the benefit of George Mason's recommendation; ". . . during the time he lived with me he had the entire Direction of the Carpenters and Joiners work of a large House; and having behaved very faithfully in my service, I can with great justice recommend him as an honest sober diligent man & I think a complete Master of the Carpenter's and Joiner's business both in theory and practice."

Buckland moved to Richmond County, Virginia, and began to diversify his skills to undertake larger projects. He worked at Mt. Airy for John Tayloe II and at Sabine Hall for Landon Carter. He worked on Montpelier (Chapter 1). Only fragments of the distinctive woodwork at Mt. Airy survive. He married, began a family, and once, in 1764, (gentleman though he was becoming) was fined ten shillings for profane swearing.

The booming city of Annapolis soon called the former London apprentice from these country mansions. He moved to the city where he was in great demand, decorating the Senate chamber of the Maryland State House and finishing the Chase-Lloyd House. He had the job of "undertaker" of the Chase-Lloyd House from 1771 to 1772, supervising the brick-work, shingling the coarser stuff. In 1773 he was replaced as the undertaker and continued only on the delicate carving. He may have been preoccupied with thoughts of the lot across the street, where he was soon to build his masterwork.

Buckland began the Hammond-Harwood House in early 1774. Charles Willson Peale began his portrait of the confident young man with a plan at his side that same year. The house was a mature design, both inside and out, with superb details and some of the finest carving anywhere. Buckland saw neither the house or the portrait completed. Forty-year-old William Buckland was dead by December. Perhaps his partner, John Randall, a former apprentice, finished the house. The Buckland portrait and his work began to gather dust.

As with most of Buckland's surviving works, the Hammond-Harwood House has been preserved as a museum. One of the finest experiences anyone can have is to follow Buckland's work through Virginia and Maryland. Begin with the exuberance of Gunston Hall. Finish your pilgrimage on the porch of the Chase-Lloyd House, and look across the street at the final masterwork of William Buckland.

ROY UNDERHILL
MASTER HOUSEWRIGHT
COLONIAL WILLIAMSBURG

Montpelier,
Prince George County,
Maryland

Text by
Ward Brown
Photographs by
Kenneth Clark
Originally published in 1930 as White Pine Monograph
Volume XVI, Number 1

General Detail of West Elevation
SNOWDEN-LONG HOUSE, LAUREL, MARYLAND

MONTPELIER, THE SNOWDEN-LONG HOUSE, PRINCE GEORGE COUNTY, MARYLAND

THE Snowden-Long House, or as it is more familiarly known to its neighbors, Montpelier, lies off the beaten track of tourist travel. Though it is one of the masterpieces of architecture, of its period and locality, it is little known outside the circle of a chosen few who have been fortunate enough to see the house.

About two miles off the main Baltimore-Washington turnpike, on a gravel road connecting Laurel and Bowie, Prince George County, Maryland, Montpelier stands on the summit of a considerable hill, surrounded by trees that almost hide it from sight. Its setting is ideal. Expansive views extend in every direction over broad acres that once heard the crooning chants of the negro slaves, at their tasks, who made possible such estates in the days when Wall Street was just a street and supporting revenues were tilled and dug from the earth with sweaty toil. It stands there today, practically unchanged except for the minor alterations necessary to make it habitable in this day and age, a monument of simple grace and sturdy strength to the skill and artistry of those who built it.

Based on the same general design and plan as other Maryland houses—the Brice and the Hammond houses of Annapolis and Whitehall,* once the home of Horatio Sharp, an early Governor of Maryland—Montpelier is individual in many respects. The interiors, particularly, have a charm of intimacy and scale that may be equaled by others but not surpassed.

The definite date of its erection is not known at any source available to the author, but it is recorded that Thomas Snowden was born here in 1751 and that the house was built by his father. Montpelier was known as the old Nicholas Snowden place to the historians of the Chesapeake Bay country. Snowden, senior, was a man of quiet, sober tastes, whose individuality was expressed in the simple exterior, devoid of useless ornament, but dignified and rather austere.

Young Thomas Snowden, is credited with adding the wings to the main house and the interior decorations which make this house so outstanding. In fact, there is a tradition to the effect that he, personally, carved the ornament in the southeast drawing room, the orig-

inal dining room. (See photographs on page 20 and 21 and measured drawings on pages 22–24.)

That the Snowdens were Quakers, and wealthy, is attested by the record that Thomas Snowden was forbidden by the fellow members of his Quaker church to come to meeting because of his great wealth and possessions. To placate them and to show that his heart was touched with the true Christian spirit, he liberated one hundred of his slaves as a peace offering and was reinstated in the good graces of his pious and perhaps envious brethren.

The grounds of Montpelier include a wonderful box garden, the number and size of whose plants is amazing. An axis at right angles to the box lined walk leading to the front door runs one hundred and forty feet parallel to the front of the house through hedges forming a miniature *pleache allée* to a garden house of wood (illustrated on pages 32–33) that is quaint in design but somehow "just right."

The exterior of Montpelier presents two almost identical elevations, facing east and west, the only difference between them being the angular plan of the wings on the east front and a more elaborate detail treatment of that doorway. The brickwork is laid in Flemish bond and is rich in color, the joints, one quarter inch wide of white mortar having the familiar trowel struck line that is used in the walls of the Hammond House. (See Chapter 3.)

The roofs, originally of shingle, have been slated and shutters have been added, which is an unusual feature of houses in this part of the country where inside blinds seem to be in universal use. The cornice, executed in wood, is detailed conventionally, but is well proportioned as a crowning member of the façade.

The window lintels are of ground brick with the mortar joints narrowed so as to be almost imperceptible.

A moulded brick water table is used in the main house and wings, but the level is not carried through, the wing base being below that of the main house.

The plan of the main house conforms in many respects to the usual Maryland *partie*, but it varies from its prototypes in having a wide hall running through the main house from front to back that gives a fine feeling of spaciousness. The vista through the front door is charm-

*This interesting house, with its beautiful and unique interiors, will be the subject of a subsequent chapter.

ing. (See page 18.) The great hedges of box form the foreground to a landscape of interest and beauty with trees, whether intentionally placed or not, coming at just the right spots to frame and finish the picture.

A well executed plaster entablature adorns the hall; its freize is ornamented with symbolic decorations of wreaths of wheat surrounding a scythe, a rake and an arrow, alternating with a fruit filled vase and the whole joined by a vine-like plant with graceful scrolls and flowers. A similar freize and cornice, though slightly varying in detail, is used around the second floor stair hall.

The staircase (page 30) has been designed and placed so that, while it forms an important part of the hall as a whole, it does not obstruct the view, since the hall is widened to receive it. It is a broad, inviting flight, facing on the second floor a wide elliptical arched opening (page 31). The details and balusters are simple in design and a wainscot continues up the stairs and around the second floor hall.

Detail of Hall Entablature
SNOWDEN-LONG HOUSE, LAUREL, MARYLAND

The feature room of the house, now known as the southeast drawing room, is an example of the design and execution of the period that is an inspiration and causes those with appreciative eyes to bless and revere the artistic sense and the superior craftsmanship of its creators. The design is not "book" architecture and though the eggs and darts, lambs tongues and all the other conventional elements are here it does not conform to the usual standards of design. One corner is cut off at forty-five degrees and here is placed a corner cupboard of unusual pattern framed by pilasters with caps carved *à la Corinthian*, by hands rather crude, but eager to decorate. The upper part of the round head doors have their muntins curiously terminated by scrolls.

There is no symmetrical wall in this room, except the south wall; no axes are acknowledged by mantel, doors, or windows; yet it has a feeling of symmetry and spacing that is most satisfactory.

The workmanship is remarkable. Mantel, trim, wainscot, china closet and cornice are all of carved wood and all are superbly executed. The whole room has been painted a lovely shade of blue which adds charm and a livable quality to the ensemble.

The northeast (page 34) and southwest (page 28) rooms on the first floor are much more simply treated with an unusually large mantel in the former and a wood paneled mantel wall in the latter.

An item of interest in the southeast and northeast rooms is that the doors on the mantel walls are only 6'-1" high, while those leading into the hall are 6'8¾". Why this was done is not entirely clear, but perhaps it seemed to the designer that it added scale and importance to the mantels. We moderns with our passion for "lining up" things have missed a few tricks by so doing and have sacrificed the very charm that these rooms possess in the quest of perfect symmetry and axial lines which look so well in plan but, as is here proved, do not count so much in actual execution.

The second floor rooms are not elaborate though each contains a well designed mantel. Really unique is the one in the northeast chamber (page 29) with its broken pediment directly over the mantel shelf and no over-mantel paneling. The coat of arms in the broken pediment is that of the present owner, but evidence was found on the wall that furnished precedent for this type of ornament.

Montpelier has been fortunate, beyond its peers, in finally falling into the hands of owners who appreciate and cherish its beauties. It has been restored sympathetically and made habitable with no apparent marring and it has been furnished throughout with a taste and discernment that make it a wonderful example of what the colonial gentleman of the eighteenth century considered a becoming dwelling place.

To Mr. and Mrs. Breckenridge Long, those present owners, are due the thanks of both author and publisher for permission to include Montpelier in this series.

East Elevation
SNOWDEN-LONG HOUSE, LAUREL, MARYLAND

East Elevation of North Wing
SNOWDEN-LONG HOUSE, LAUREL, MARYLAND

West Elevation of Main House

SNOWDEN-LONG HOUSE, LAUREL, MARYLAND

East Doorway
SNOWDEN-LONG HOUSE, LAUREL, MARYLAND

West Doorway
SNOWDEN-LONG HOUSE, LAUREL, MARYLAND

View Through East Doorway
SNOWDEN-LONG HOUSE, LAUREL, MARYLAND

First Floor Hall
SNOWDEN-LONG HOUSE, LAUREL, MARYLAND

Southeast Drawing Room, China Closet
SNOWDEN-LONG HOUSE, LAUREL, MARYLAND

Corner of Southeast Drawing Room, Formerly the Dining Room
SNOWDEN-LONG HOUSE, LAUREL, MARYLAND

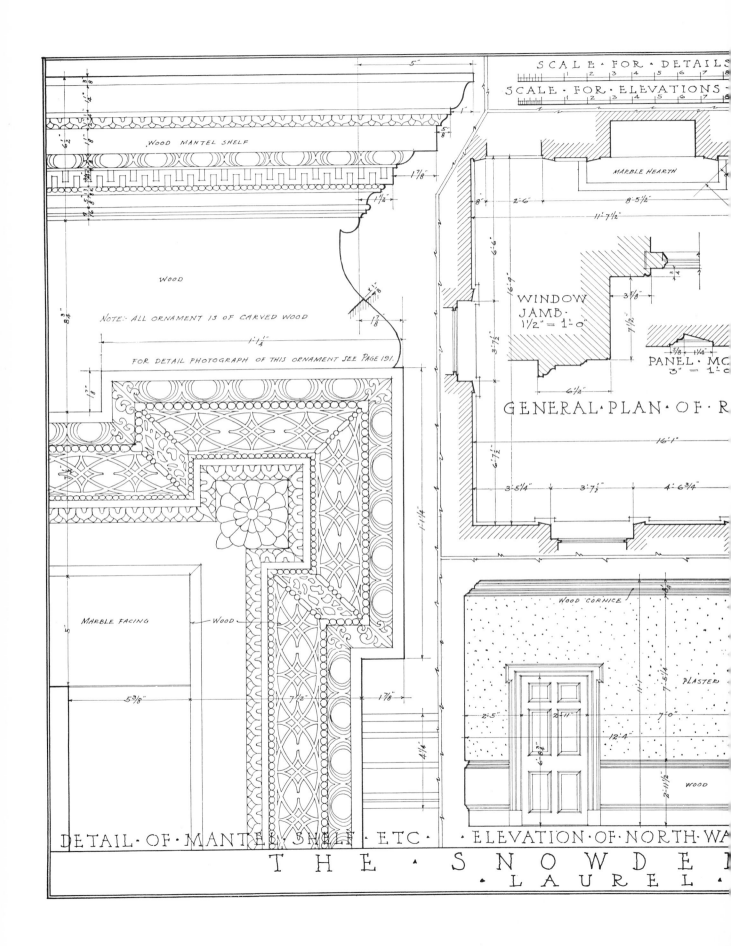

WOOD MANTEL SHELF

5"

WOOD

NOTE:- ALL ORNAMENT IS OF CARVED WOOD

FOR DETAIL PHOTOGRAPH OF THIS ORNAMENT SEE PAGE 191.

MARBLE FACING

WOOD

MARBLE HEARTH

WINDOW
JAMB·
1½" = 1'-0"

PANEL · MO
3" = 1'-0

GENERAL · PLAN · OF · R

16'-1"

3'-5¼"   3'-7½"   4'-6¾"

WOOD CORNICE

PLASTER

WOOD

DETAIL · OF · MANTEL · SHELF · ETC ·   · ELEVATION · OF · NORTH · WA

THE · SNOWDEN

· LAUREL ·

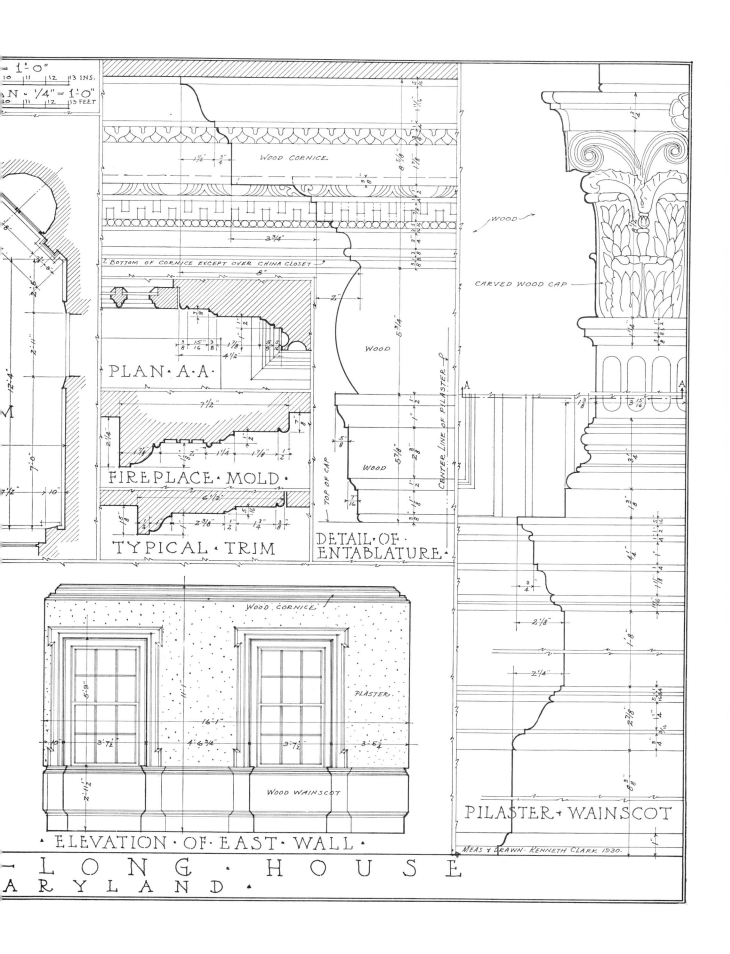

WOOD CORNICE

PLAN·A·A·

FIREPLACE·MOLD·

TYPICAL·TRIM

DETAIL·OF·ENTABLATURE·

Bottom of cornice except over china closet

WOOD

TOP OF CAP

CENTER LINE OF PILASTER

WOOD

CARVED WOOD CAP

PILASTER·+·WAINSCOT

WOOD CORNICE

PLASTER·

WOOD WAINSCOT

·ELEVATION·OF·EAST·WALL·

MEAS + DRAWN · KENNETH CLARK · 1930.

·LONG·HOUSE·

·ARYLAND·

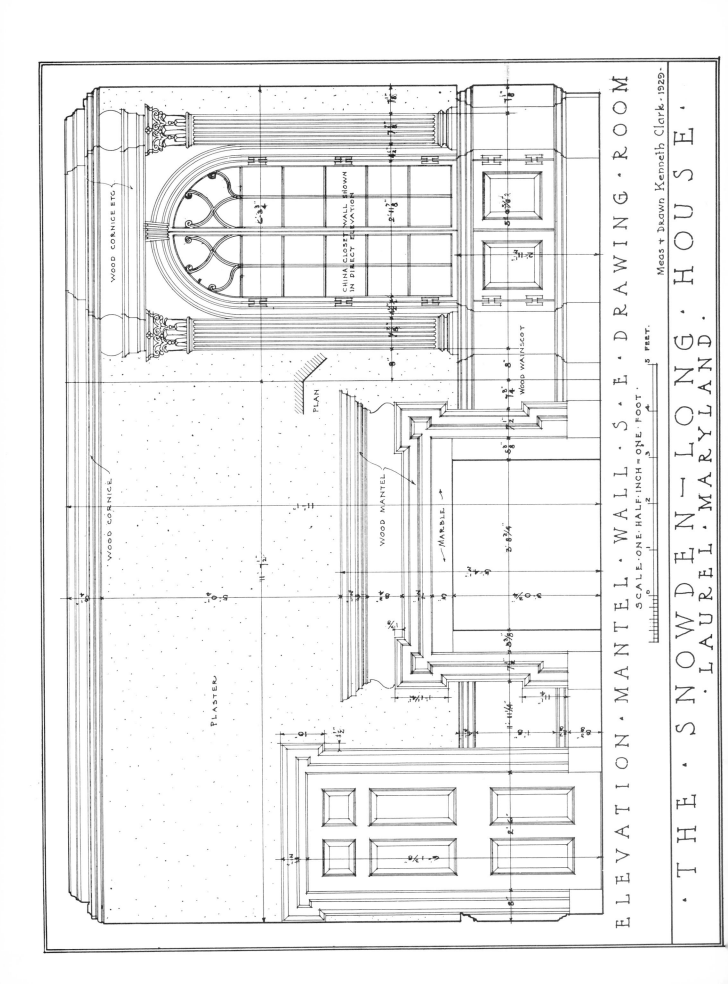

· ELEVATION · MANTEL · WALL · S · E · DRAWING · ROOM ·

SCALE · ONE · HALF · INCH = ONE · FOOT

· THE · SNOWDEN ~ LONG · HOUSE ·
· LAUREL · MARYLAND ·

Meas + Drawn Kenneth Clark · 1929 ·

WOOD CORNICE ETC.

CHINA CLOSET WALL SHOWN
IN DIRECT ELEVATION

WOOD WAINSCOT

PLAN

WOOD CORNICE

WOOD MANTEL

MARBLE

PLASTER

Southeast Drawing Room, Mantel Wall
SNOWDEN-LONG HOUSE, LAUREL, MARYLAND

Detail of Southeast Drawing Room Entablature
SNOWDEN-LONG HOUSE, LAUREL, MARYLAND

Detail of Southeast Drawing Room Mantel
SNOWDEN-LONG HOUSE, LAUREL, MARYLAND

Southwest Room, First Floor
SNOWDEN-LONG HOUSE, LAUREL, MARYLAND

Northeast Bedroom Mantel
SNOWDEN-LONG HOUSE, LAUREL, MARYLAND

Stairway Detail
SNOWDEN-LONG HOUSE, LAUREL, MARYLAND

Second Floor Hall
SNOWDEN-LONG HOUSE, LAUREL, MARYLAND

Garden House of Montpelier
SNOWDEN-LONG HOUSE, LAUREL, MARYLAND

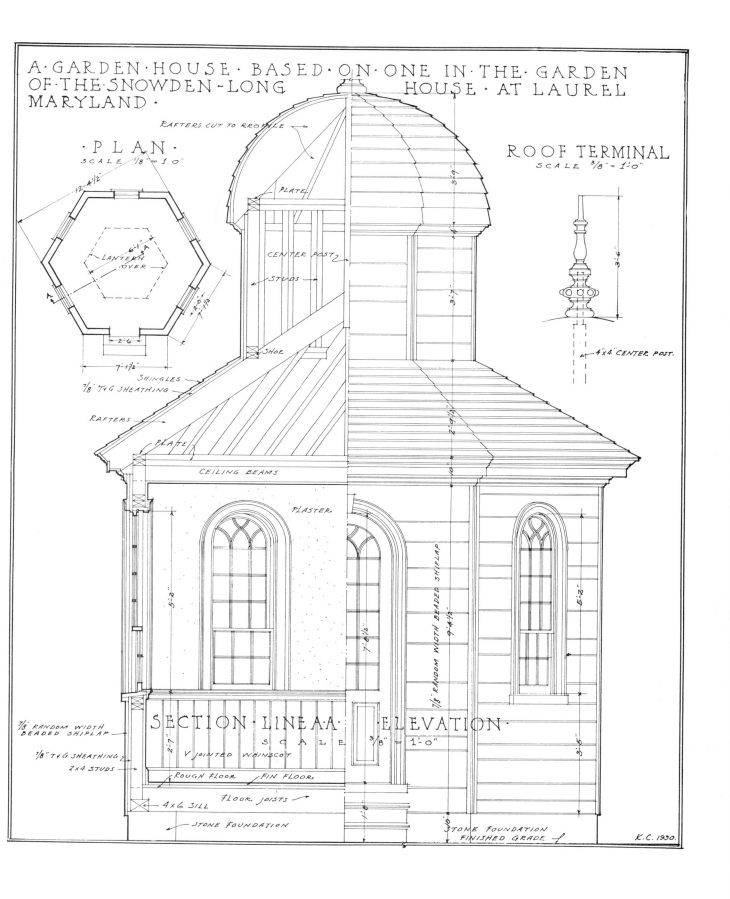

A·GARDEN·HOUSE·BASED·ON·ONE·IN·THE·GARDEN·OF·THE·SNOWDEN-LONG HOUSE·AT·LAUREL MARYLAND·

·PLAN·
SCALE '⅛" = 1·0'

12' 4½"

LANTERN OVER

2'-6"

7' 1½"

ROOF TERMINAL
SCALE ⅜" = 1'-0"

3'-6"

4"x4" CENTER POST.

RAFTERS CUT TO RROFILE

PLATE

CENTER POST

STUDS

SHOE

SHINGLES

⅞" T+G SHEATHING

RAFTERS

PLATE

CEILING BEAMS

PLASTER

3'-4"

3'-7"

2'-7½"

10"

7'-6½"

9'-4½"

⅞" RANDOM WIDTH BEADED SHIPLAP

5'-2"

5'-2"

3'-6"

⅞" RANDOM WIDTH BEADED SHIPLAP

⅞" T+G SHEATHING

2x4 STUDS

4x6 SILL

STONE FOUNDATION

2'-7"

V JOINTED WAINSCOT

ROUGH FLOOR

FIN FLOOR

FLOOR JOISTS

1'-6"

10"

STONE FOUNDATION
FINISHED GRADE

SECTION·LINE·AA··ELEVATION·
SCALE ⅜" = 1'-0"

K.C. 1930.

Northeast Room, First Floor
SNOWDEN-LONG HOUSE, LAUREL, MARYLAND

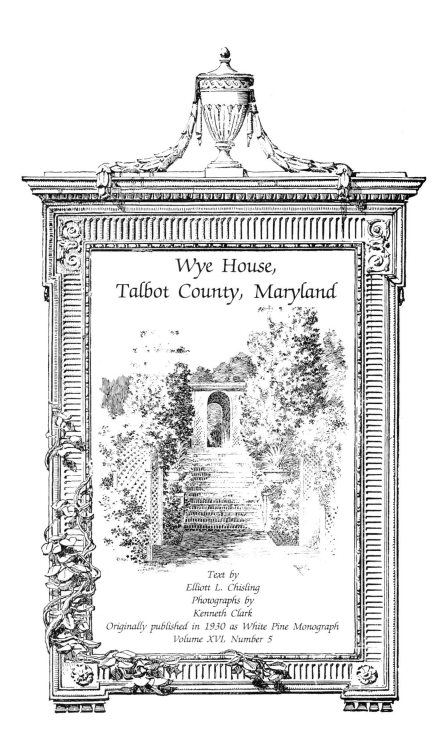

Wye House,
Talbot County, Maryland

Text by
Elliott L. Chisling
Photographs by
Kenneth Clark
Originally published in 1930 as White Pine Monograph
Volume XVI, Number 5

Orangery
WYE HOUSE, TALBOT COUNTY, MARYLAND

WYE HOUSE, TALBOT COUNTY, MARYLAND

IN Talbot County, Maryland, situated on the westerly bank of the Front Wye River, and approximately midway between Easton and Clarebourne, is an estate which combines rare historic value with an architectural interest that places it in a class with the great residences of our early aristocratic land owners. To many, this great acreage is known as the Lloyds Estate, while others refer to the location as Wye House, the home of the Lloyds for eight generations.

Existing records tell us that Edward Lloyd the first came to the colony of Virginia from Wales in 1623 and was a burgess in the Virginia Assembly which met at "Preston-on-Patuxent" (Charlesgift). It was Edward Lloyd the first, who in 1662 built the original residence known as Wye House, upon a tract of land estimated to have been five thousand acres. Although this house stood for over one hundred years, there are no records whatsoever of it.

On the night of March 13, 1781, an incendiary fire burned the original Wye House and during the conflagration all of the historic records of the Lloyd family, the family treasures and plate disappeared. Only a small part of the original Wye House remained standing and today this is used as an outbuilding.

Available records indicate that the present Wye House was rebuilt by Edward Lloyd the fourth, immediately after the original house was destroyed. He succeeded in erecting a most charming colonial residence which seems to have been planned not only as a residence, but as a pivot or key building to a great estate. Other features of the general plan followed in a most capable manner. An observer will note the careful arrangement of all the buildings.

Comparatively few sightseers have visited Wye House, for the estate is not easily accessible and not open to the public. That may also account for the fact that Wye House is not well known to students of Colonial architecture, except those who may reside in that particular locality. Furthermore, the casual tourist who may use the secondary roadway which passes its gates, will not see any part of Wye House or its buildings for the reason that they are set back approximately three-quarters of a mile from the roadway. One must be carefully directed to its location, which is marked by a pair of great wrought iron gates which were brought from Italy by a later Lloyd and erected as the entrance to this great estate. These gates are kept locked and bolted and this entry is no longer used. The driveway to Wye House has not been preserved and nature has converted it into a grassy lane that stretches away in the distance for nearly three-quarters of a mile. The sheep that are kept at Wye have wisely chosen what remains of this roadway as a pasturing place and, if one can for a moment forget its present appearance, the former grandeur and elegance of the main approach to Wye House can be appreciated. Magnificent trees still flank both sides of the roadway and form an arboreal passage worthy of Versailles. Entry to the estate is now made by a service roadway which passes the old slave quarters.

At the end of the main driveway stands the present Wye House. This building is of two stories and includes a long hall from the entry porch to the porch on the rear, a drawing room, parlor, dining room and chambers. One story wings, connected by corridors, contain a library on one side and service rooms on the other. In all, it presents a pleasing façade of approximately two hundred feet. The exterior shows a simple and dignified treatment of siding with shuttered windows, except for the central three light window over the entrance porch which is ornamented by pilasters and entablature. The main roof, roofs of side wings and entrance porch were originally shingled but are now of slate, and in elevation are pediments of flush boarding retaining the same roof pitch throughout. The entrance motif consists of two columns and two pilasters on the front and flush boarding on the sides, pierced by circular headed openings. Stone steps, enclosed by hedges, complete this central motif. There is no carving on the exterior. In fact this simplicity of treatment is carried out in the interior of the house, where one still finds cornices, arches, pilasters, architraves, paneling and trim of simple profiles. Charming mantels set off these rooms, though none of them contain more than a carved bead or fret. The doors are fitted with exquisite hardware in silver, brass and wrought iron that was undoubtedly made and brought from England. One cannot forget the furnishings of Wye House. The rooms are full of rare colonial furniture and pictures, vases and cameos, andirons and fireplace implements, lamps and candelabra, firearms and dozens of other things. There are many priceless framed parchments of great historic value and aside from its beauty as a colonial relic, Wye House is literally a museum. Fortunately, this fine collection of antiques has not been allowed to fall into the hands of collectors.

On the rear of the house is a colonnaded open porch facing a great rectangular lawn which in turn is enclosed on each side by beautiful boxwood hedges and trees that only age and good care could produce. At one end of the lawn and facing directly the rear of the house is the Orangery. To behold the Orangery from the porch in its frame of lawn, sky and trees at each side is to gaze at a picture perfect in its composition. The first impression to both layman and student of architecture is pleasing beyond words. Invariably a closer inspection is desired and one walks down the great lawn to examine what may easily be considered a perfect example of Georgian design. The building is unusual in its simplicity and perfection. It is two stories flanked on both sides by one story wings of equal proportions. The roofs are shingled. The lower half of the two story center is rusticated stonework. Rusticated stone quoins continue on the corners to the roof. One will receive a great surprise to discover that what seems to be four flat arches with wedge-shaped voussoirs over the four large windows are nothing more than wood lintels, hewn and carved to carry out the treatment of stone rustications below. Time and weather have almost succeeded in blending these wood lintels into the general color of the building. The upper story is of brick, stuccoed, and the side wings are of the same materials. The beauty of this building reveals the work of a great architect and the cooperation of capable craftsmen.

As far as is known, the Orangery was built shortly after the present Wye House and was used to house plants and shrubs during the winter months. Since that time, the Orangery has served many purposes principally that of storehouse. Without a doubt, this building is unsurpassed in this country and should be preserved as an historic example of Georgian architecture.

The interest of Wye House, which tends to increase from the moment of passing the front gates and seems to have reached its peak after seeing the Orangery, is not at an end. There still remains the family burying plot, the last resting place of the Lloyds who have passed on during the three centuries that have elapsed. This is located at the rear of the Orangery. In a book called *Historic Graves of Maryland and the District of Columbia* by Helen W. Ridgeley, the author gives an interesting

account of the Wye burial plot, which begins by saying: "On account of its age and of the prominent people buried there and also because of the beauty of its tombs and their quaint inscriptions, the old Lloyd burying ground at Wye, the home of the Lloyds since 1660, is the most interesting in Maryland. . . . The family badge of a lion rampant, appears on variously carved shields." Here also are the unmarked graves of those who died and were buried before Col. Philemon Lloyd, who died in 1685. His is the oldest stone with the exception of one inscribed to the memory of Capt. Strong of Stephney, in the County of Middlesex, who died in 1684. There are no records available of the Lloyd connection to Captain Strong. Close to Col. Philemon Lloyd, is buried his wife who died in 1697 and his three daughters. Much can be written about those buried at Wye, particularly the historically famous members of the family who died in the service of their country and who are now recorded in the archives of our history.

There are other interesting buildings and quaint details. There are the smokehouse and the old slave quarters and more recent additions, all comprising a small village in itself. One can still see the colored folk going quietly about their chores, the major part of which consists of caring for the grounds and landscaping around the house and Orangery. A rare old U-shaped brick gutter leads away from the house. Last, but not least, are the brick walls enclosing the gardens and burial plot. These are of hand-made brick with sloping copings of the same material. The walls are pierced by arched openings where paths occur. Covered with vines and moss, and overhung by trees, these walls help complete the perfect picture.

It is difficult to do justice to the beauty of this estate by any written description. One can appreciate it only by a personal visit. Fortunately, Wye House still remains in the possession of the present generation of Lloyds and is occupied by a Lloyd, Mrs. J. Addison Singer, to whom the author of this chapter and the publishers owe their thanks and appreciation for having been permitted to visit Wye House and for the hospitality shown them.

There are few estates in America today which exemplify the complete requirements necessary to the conduct of what was a community in itself. Mt. Vernon is one and Wye House another. They were self-sustaining in almost every particular and both have the various outbuildings which the many trades and crafts required. Wye House can teach us much of the life lived by its early owners who combined culture with the rugged determination on which was built the foundations of our present government.

South Façade
WYE HOUSE, TALBOT COUNTY, MARYLAND

South Façade

WYE HOUSE—c1780—TALBOT COUNTY, MARYLAND

FIRST WYE HOUSE—1662—TALBOT COUNTY, MARYLAND
Only part of original house still standing.

Porch Detail, Rear Elevation
WYE HOUSE, TALBOT COUNTY, MARYLAND

Side Elevation With Unique Gutter
WYE HOUSE, TALBOT COUNTY, MARYLAND

Dining Room
WYE HOUSE, TALBOT COUNTY, MARYLAND

Hall
WYE HOUSE, TALBOT COUNTY, MARYLAND

Detail of Orangery, South Façade
WYE HOUSE, TALBOT COUNTY, MARYLAND

Orangery, South Façade
WYE HOUSE, TALBOT COUNTY, MARYLAND

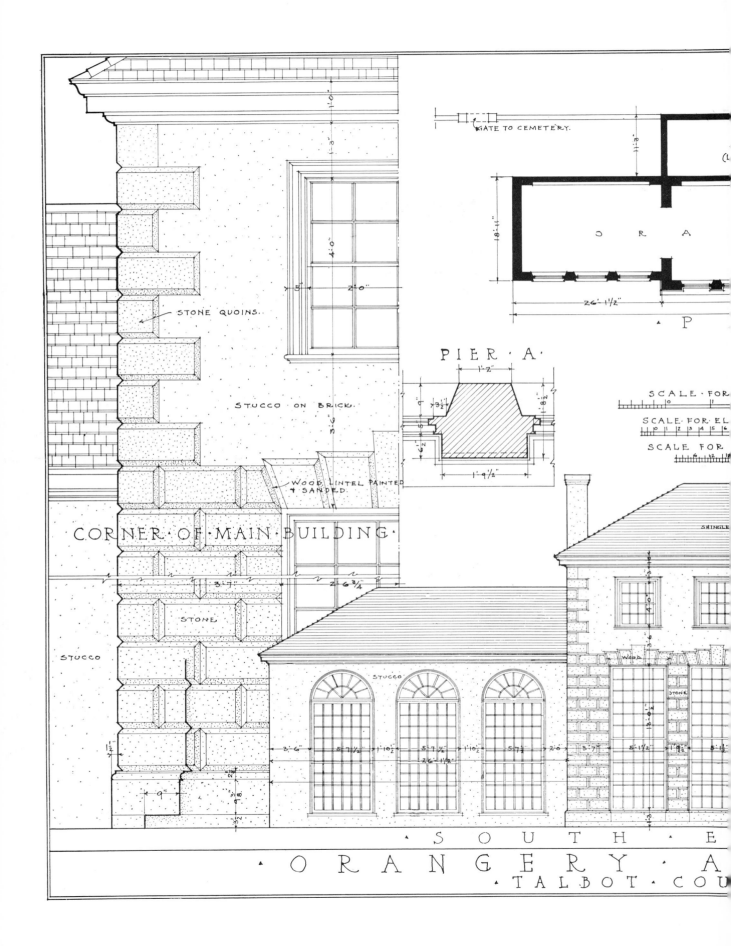

GATE TO CEMETERY.

26'-1½"

PIER · A ·

STONE QUOINS.

STUCCO · ON · BRICK.

WOOD · LINTEL · PAINTED
+ SANDED.

CORNER · OF · MAIN · BUILDING ·

STONE

STUCCO

SCALE · FOR

SCALE · FOR · EL

SCALE · FOR

SHINGLE

WOOD

STUCCO

STONE

· S O U T H · E

· O R A N G E R Y · A

· T A L B O T · C O U

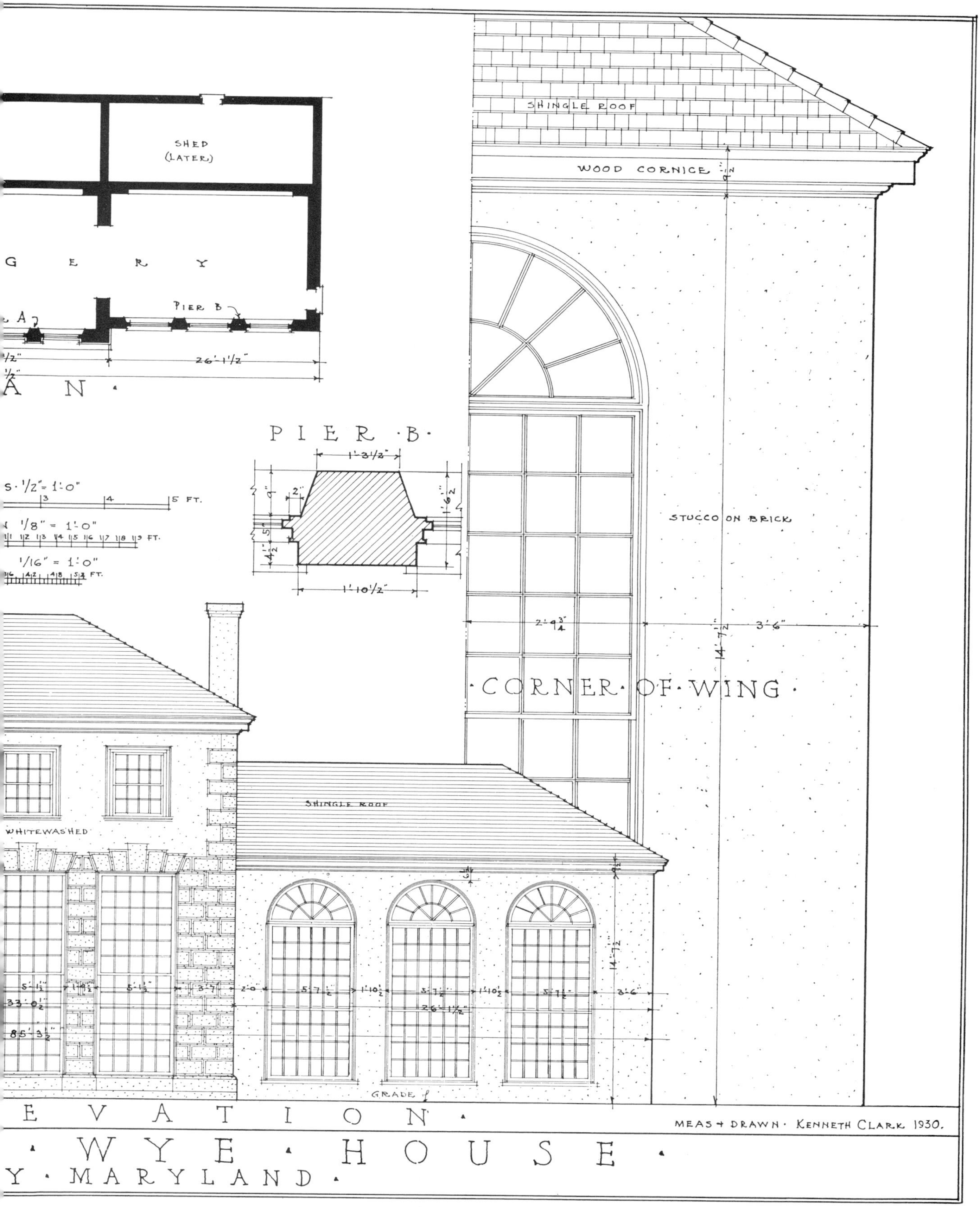

SHED
(LATER)

G E R Y

PIER B

A

26'-1½"

N

PIER · B ·

1'-3½"

1'-10½"

2'-9¾"

s ½" = 1'0"
1'/8" = 1'0"
1/16" = 1'0"

SHINGLE ROOF

WOOD CORNICE

STUCCO ON BRICK

3'-6"

14'-7"

CORNER · OF · WING ·

WHITEWASHED

SHINGLE ROOF

5'-1½" 1'-9½" 5'-1½" 3'-7½" 2'-0 5'-7½" 1'-10½" 3'-7½" 1'-10½" 5'-7½" 3'-6"

33'-0½"

85'-3½"

26'-1½"

14'-7½"

GRADE

MEAS + DRAWN · KENNETH CLARK · 1930 ·

E V A T I O N ·

· W Y E · H O U S E ·

Y · M A R Y L A N D ·

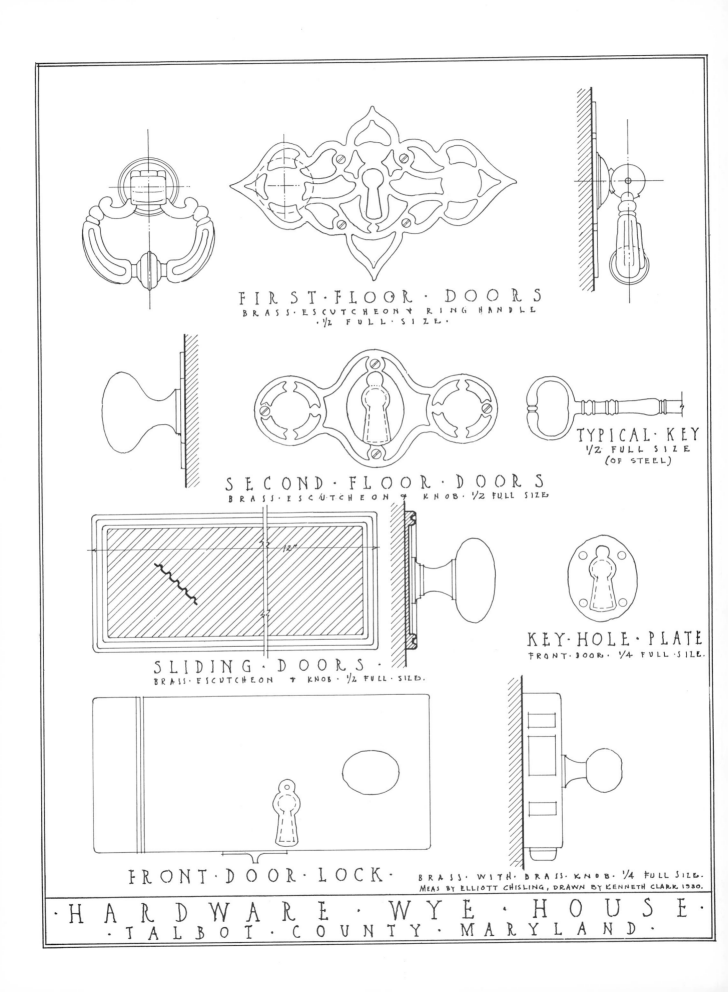

FIRST·FLOOR·DOORS
BRASS·ESCUTCHEON & RING HANDLE
·½ FULL·SIZE·

SECOND·FLOOR·DOORS
BRASS·ESCUTCHEON & KNOB·½ FULL SIZE

TYPICAL·KEY
½ FULL SIZE
(OF STEEL)

SLIDING·DOORS·
BRASS·ESCUTCHEON & KNOB·½ FULL·SIZE.

KEY·HOLE·PLATE
FRONT·DOOR·¼ FULL·SIZE.

FRONT·DOOR·LOCK·
BRASS·WITH·BRASS·KNOB·¼ FULL·SIZE.
MEAS BY ELLIOTT CHISLING, DRAWN BY KENNETH CLARK 1930.

·HARDWARE·WYE·HOUSE·
·TALBOT·COUNTY·MARYLAND·

Escutcheon and Handle, First Floor Doors

Escutcheon and Knob, First Floor Sliding Doors
HARDWARE—WYE HOUSE, TALBOT COUNTY, MARYLAND

Parlor

WYE HOUSE, TALBOT COUNTY, MARYLAND

Drawing Room From Dining Room
WYE HOUSE, TALBOT COUNTY, MARYLAND

Drawing Room Mantel
WYE HOUSE, TALBOT COUNTY, MARYLAND

WYE HOUSE, TALBOT COUNTY, MARYLAND

Reception Room
WYE HOUSE, TALBOT COUNTY, MARYLAND

Stair Detail
WYE HOUSE, TALBOT COUNTY, MARYLAND

Entrance Porch
WYE HOUSE—1782—TALBOT COUNTY, MARYLAND

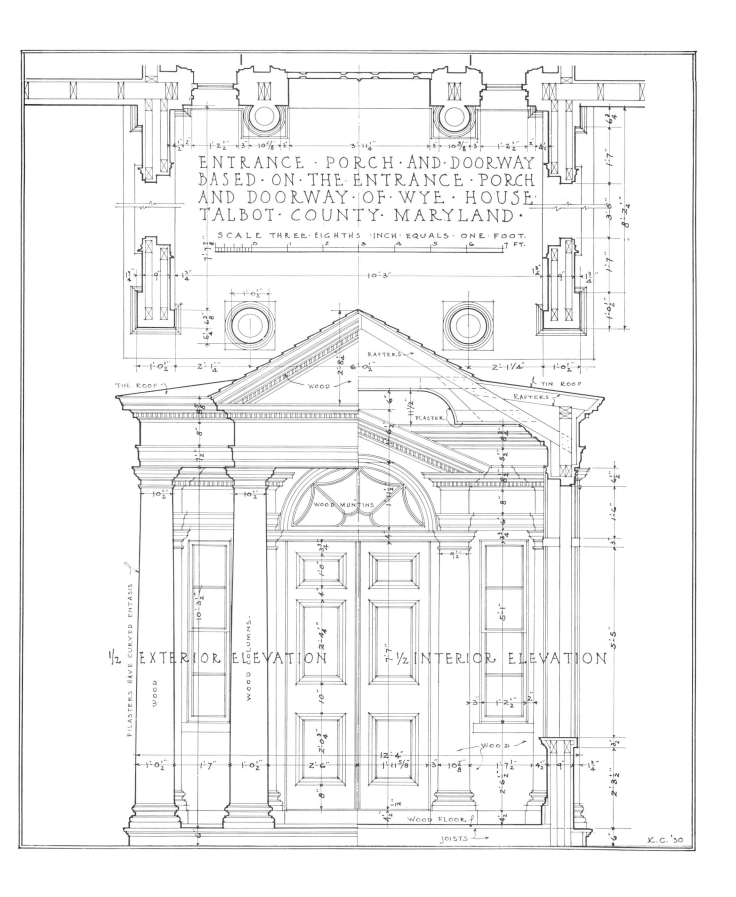

ENTRANCE · PORCH · AND · DOORWAY
BASED · ON · THE · ENTRANCE · PORCH
AND · DOORWAY · OF · WYE · HOUSE ·
TALBOT · COUNTY · MARYLAND ·

SCALE · THREE · EIGHTHS · INCH · EQUALS · ONE · FOOT.

0 1 2 3 4 5 6 7 FT.

TIN. ROOF

RAFTERS

WOOD

TIN. ROOF

RAFTERS

PLASTER

WOOD MUNTINS

PILASTERS HAVE CURVED ENTASIS

WOOD

WOOD COLUMNS.

½ EXTERIOR ELEVATION   ½ INTERIOR ELEVATION

WOOD

WOOD FLOOR

JOISTS

K. G. '30

Wall Enclosing the Burial Plot and Gardens
WYE HOUSE, HOME OF THE LLOYDS, TALBOT COUNTY, MARYLAND

Matthias Hammond House,
Annapolis, Maryland,
Part One

Text by
Effingham C. Desmond
Photographs by
Kenneth Clark
Originally published in 1929 as White Pine Monograph
Volume XV, Number 4

PORTRAIT OF MATTHEW BUCKLAND, ARCHITECT
Painted by Peale for Matthias Hammond

A PRE-REVOLUTIONARY ANNAPOLIS HOUSE: MATTHIAS HAMMOND HOUSE, BUILT 1770–1774, MATTHEW BUCKLAND, ARCHITECT, PART ONE

IT is not strange that Annapolis, the capital of the state of Maryland, should bear stamped unmistakably upon its ancient buildings the image of the highest Georgian standards of the architecture of the mother country, England, for this "colonial" city was perhaps more intimately related to and kept in closer touch with its national progenitor than any other on this continent. Its people were substantial, wealthy and aristocratic, their thoughts and actions bespoke England rather than the rugged infant nucleus that was one day destined to become this United States of America. The Annopolitans of the eighteenth century were not hard fisted pioneers, fighting a wilderness for a precarious existence, but rather the finished result of those pioneers' efforts, a settled community of sophisticated citizens, living an English life in everything but locale.

They had their theatres and clubs, their servants and their coaches and fours; among them were lawyers, doctors and architects. The professions were liberally practiced and the rich men of the colony could afford to use such service. Indeed wealth in this city was almost up to the later standards set by our captains of industry, for men like Charles Carroll and others were owners of substantial businesses and properties that today would dub them by that title. Such citizens were content with nothing but the best things in life and the houses they built to live in were a reflection of their condition and their age.

Annapolis is rich in examples of the best in domestic architecture of the period and perhaps the one outstanding house of the many is that which has been chosen as the subject of this chapter. In 1770, Matthias Hammond, a lawyer and planter, being interested in taking to himself a mate to share his fortune and his home, began its construction.

He engaged as architect one Matthew Buckland who hailed, tradition says, from Philadelphia and who was efficient enough to impress upon his client the substantial merit of his work; that he was appreciated there is definite evidence for his portrait painted by Peale and

executed at the order of Hammond was destined to grace the walls of his masterpiece for many years, and hangs there today mute evidence that his genius carved for itself a niche well worthy of commemoration.

Evidences of his command of design are strongly apparent elsewhere in Annapolis, but the Hammond House is the culmination of his efforts and stands today as one of the finest, if not the finest, example of the work of the Colonial period.

For years the interior of this house was inaccessible to visitors and though many attempts have been made by architects and students to penetrate beyond the closed doors none were more than partially successful until a short time ago, when, the owner having died, the property was thrown upon the market and purchased by St. John's College to insure its preservation and to house a colonial museum. The ultimate ambition of those interested is to restore the furnishings and hangings to the perfection of its greatest days and this movement has already progressed to the point where one can realize that the work is being done by knowing and understanding souls.

Among them, and most active in the actual work of restoration is Mr. R. T. Halsey, formerly of the Metropolitan Museum of New York and now of the faculty of St. John's College. To him the writer of this chapter and the editor of The Monograph Series owe a debt of gratitude. His courtesy made the task of recording the work a pleasure and the house both inside and out was put at their disposal freely and without condition.

Situated on the corner at the crossing of King George Street and Maryland Avenue, the house occupies a block front and the outer dimensions of its plan are approximately 131 feet x 46 feet. The façade presents a two story main house and wings connected by one story links. Its principal exterior characteristics are dignity and simplicity relieved by the elaborate and beautifully carved wood doorway with window over, a cornice and pediment window. The ornament is concentrated in

Editor's Note: See preface for information on architect Matthew Buckland as William Buckland.

these details and thereby serves to accentuate the massiveness of the large areas of brickwork. The lintels are flat brick arches and the base or water table is of moulded brick. The band course between first and second story windows and the water table have been laid with practically no joint, in contrast with the rest of the wall surfaces and the lack of the vertical lines in those members gives them a horizontality that was undoubtedly a deliberate and foreseen result of the architect's study. The brick units average 8″ x 4″ x 2⅜″ and the joints, of white mortar, are not more than ¼″ in thickness. An interesting detail, that seems to give quite a "sparkle" to the texture of the walls, is the fact that the mason after striking the joint practically flush has drawn a line, evidently using a straightedge and his trowel point, in the middle of each joint, both horizontal and vertical and this treatment tends to eliminate the apparentness of many irregularities caused by variations in the brick shapes. The chimneys are square in plan and are topped out with a simple brick coping. The window reveals are uniformly 4″ and in the central bay of the front elevation the additional thickness of wall required for the break has been added to the window frame outside, making the inside reveal, which comes in the same room as a window in the thinner wall, the same.

The brick is rich, dull salmon in color, laid in Flemish bond and the present surface texture is about that of the usual run of modern unselected "common."

The garden — or rear — façade follows the front identically as to general proportions, but the main house is broken by a treatment of four brick pilasters with a full cornice, frieze and architrave of wood above them and the pediment and its decorated window is repeated.

The plan has many clever and ingenious features: The right-hand wing, looking from the street, is a kitchen and service portion and the left-hand one, an office wing for the original owner's use. This wing does not connect with the main house by an interior door, but is entered only through the link by the front and the garden doors.

The main house plan is unconventional in many ways, but is a finished architectural study with all axes, etc., so necessary to the success of a formal, symmetrical house of this type, properly considered and worked out. The stairway, contrary to the usual procedure, is not made a feature of the entrance hall, but is relegated to one side in a separate space, leaving the entrance hall a perfectly symmetrical room as to openings, etc. A door opens directly opposite the front door into the "big" room of the house, called the state dining room and is on axis with the door to the garden. The uses of the minor rooms are doubtful. They have been marked on the plan, as "drawing room" and "reception room." It is possible that the rear drawing room served the family as dining room on other than state occasions, but nothing warrants this conclusion except its location. Perhaps life in this mansion made every meal a ceremony, whether attended by guests or not and worthy of the magnificent setting the state dining room provides. The treatment of the minor rooms on the first floor is simple, each has a fine mantel, wainscot and cornice, each room treated individually without repetition of design.

The woodwork of the interiors of this house is its most remarkable feature. The use of the material and its ornamental treatment by the architect and his craftsmen are worthy of separate consideration and will be the subject of the succeeding chapter.

The second floor plan repeats the first exactly as to spaces, the room over the state dining room being a ballroom treated in an Adamesque style with a garlanded mantel and fluted cornice with urn ornaments at intervals. The space above the second floor ceiling is not finished off, but left merely as an attic ventilated by the two pediment windows, which relieved the architect from the necessity of breaking the roof with dormers, the absence of which helps the repose and simplicity of the elevations.

On the west wall of the main house is an arched window, lighting the stair hall, which is treated with a quoined trim that appears rather heavy in contrast with the delicacy of the other details.

The whole exterior scheme seems wonderfully consistent and logical. The method of linking wings and main house by passages opening on both the street and garden front gives access to the servants' portion and the office wing without disturbing the occupants of the main house. Formerly, when the Hammond property was of far greater compass than the present lot, the rear elevation looked out upon a garden of generous proportions. The only remainder of this former grandeur is some fine box, which now grows almost on the line of a neighboring house that in these surroundings shocks by its modern utilitarian ugliness.

In the height of its glory the Hammond House was a true example of an American gentleman's home where he lived a life of refinement, surrounded by a setting that could do nothing but intensify the spirit of hospitality and good will that flowed within its walls. It stands today a living example of great architecture that we who run and rush may read and absorb some of its beauties and the methods by which they were achieved. "Modern" movements may come and go but such work as this is never old or new. It stands, as all the classics of our arts stand, self-sufficient and complete.

Detail of Street Façade
MATTHIAS HAMMOND HOUSE, ANNAPOLIS, MARYLAND

Street Façade
MATTHIAS HAMMOND HOUSE, ANNAPOLIS, MARYLAND

Garden Façade

MATTHIAS HAMMOND HOUSE, ANNAPOLIS, MARYLAND

Detail of Central Bay, Street Façade
MATTHIAS HAMMOND HOUSE, ANNAPOLIS, MARYLAND

Detail of Central Bay, Garden Façade
MATTHIAS HAMMOND HOUSE, ANNAPOLIS, MARYLAND

Detail of Cornice, Garden Façade
MATTHIAS HAMMOND HOUSE, ANNAPOLIS, MARYLAND

Detail of Pediment and Cartouche, Garden Façade
MATTHIAS HAMMOND HOUSE, ANNAPOLIS, MARYLAND

Detail of Link Between Main House and Wing, Street Façade
MATTHIAS HAMMOND HOUSE, ANNAPOLIS, MARYLAND

Garden Façade

MATTHIAS HAMMOND HOUSE, ANNAPOLIS, MARYLAND

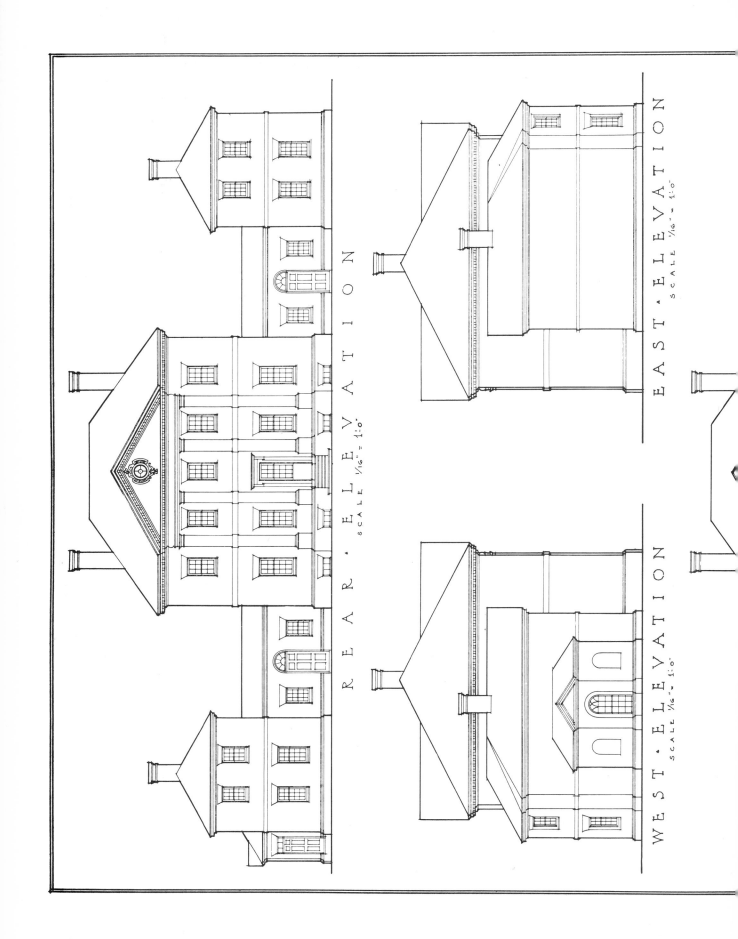

R E A R · E L E V A T I O N

SCALE ⅟₁₆" = 1'·0"

E A S T · E L E V A T I O N

SCALE ⅟₁₆" = 1'·0"

W E S T · E L E V A T I O N

SCALE ⅟₁₆" = 1'·0"

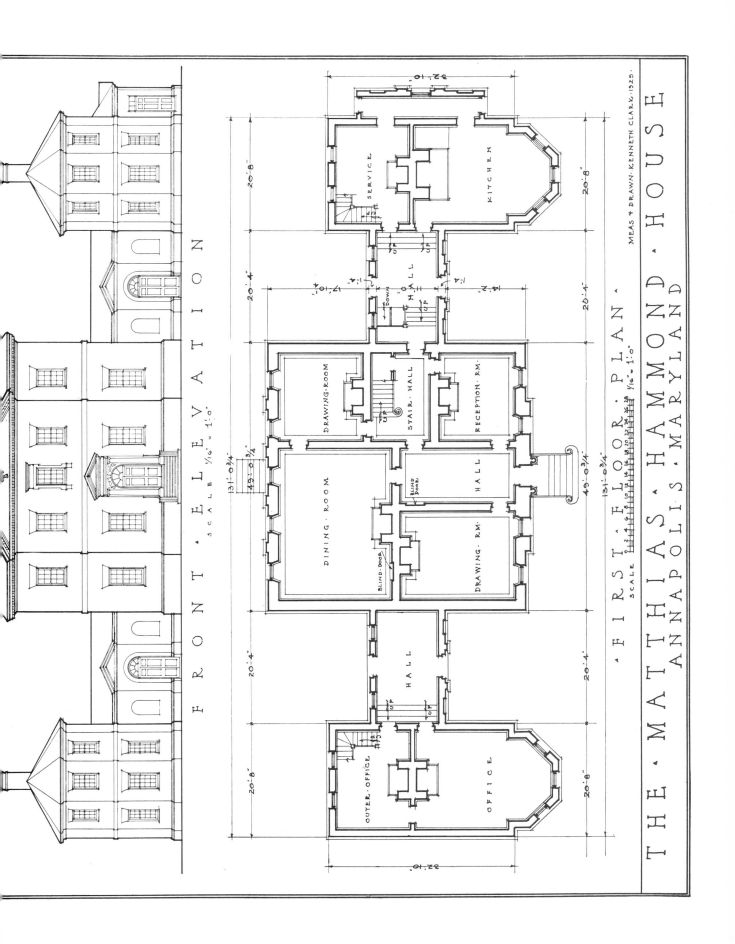

FRONT ELEVATION
SCALE ⅛" = 1'0"

FIRST FLOOR PLAN
SCALE ⅛" = 1'0"

MEAS + DRAWN KENNETH CLARK 1925

THE MATTHIAS HAMMOND HOUSE
ANNAPOLIS MARYLAND

MEAS + DRAWN KENNETH CLARK '29.

· THE · MATTHIAS · HAMMOND · HOUSE ·
· ANNAPOLIS · MARYLAND ·

Detail of Main Entrance, Street Façade
MATTHIAS HAMMOND HOUSE, ANNAPOLIS, MARYLAND

Detail of Main Entrance Doorway Entablature, Street Façade
MATTHIAS HAMMOND HOUSE, ANNAPOLIS, MARYLAND

Detail of Garden Doorway Entablature, Garden Façade
MATTHIAS HAMMOND HOUSE, ANNAPOLIS, MARYLAND

Detail of Stairway Window
MATTHIAS HAMMOND HOUSE, ANNAPOLIS, MARYLAND

Detail of Second Story Hall Window, Street Façade
MATTHIAS HAMMOND HOUSE, ANNAPOLIS, MARYLAND

Garden Doorway
MATTHIAS HAMMOND HOUSE, ANNAPOLIS, MARYLAND

Link Between Main House and Wing
MATTHIAS HAMMOND HOUSE, ANNAPOLIS, MARYLAND

Elevation of West Wing
MATTHIAS HAMMOND HOUSE, ANNAPOLIS, MARYLAND

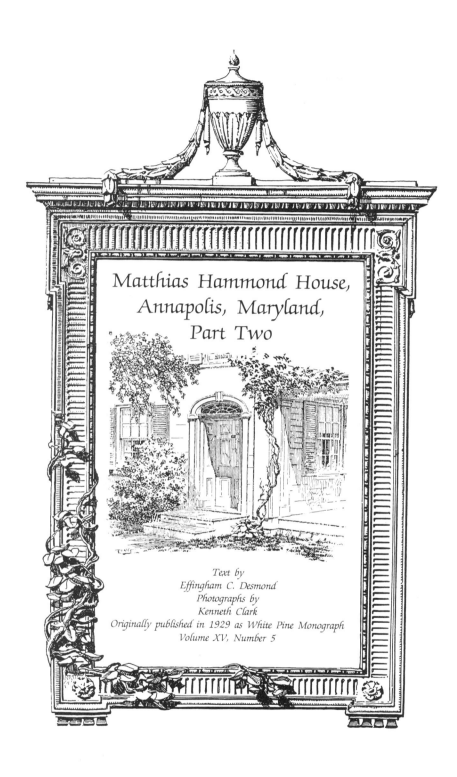

Matthias Hammond House, Annapolis, Maryland, Part Two

Text by
Effingham C. Desmond
Photographs by
Kenneth Clark
Originally published in 1929 as White Pine Monograph
Volume XV, Number 5

Dining Room
MATTHIAS HAMMOND HOUSE, ANNAPOLIS, MARYLAND
Matthew Buckland, Architect

MATTHIAS HAMMOND HOUSE, PART TWO

THE Hammond-Harwood House, the exterior of which is illustrated in the preceding chapter, adds much to the charm of old Annapolis, a charm which grows on one with every visit, for it is our one Georgian town unscarred by factory or huge apartment houses. True, many of the minor houses there are of the pre-Civil War period when the increasing needs of the Naval Academy necessitated more buildings in the town. Simple and purely utilitarian, they afford a satisfactory setting for the eight superb eighteenth-century houses which remain to bear eloquent testimony to the love of the beautiful which existed there during the trying days preceding the American Revolution. Annapolitans justly take pride in the fact that three of these great mansions were lived in by signers of the Declaration of Independence, Charles Carroll, Samuel Chase, and William Paca.

The house we are discussing was built by Matthias Hammond, a most active Son of Liberty and leader in the patriot cause. What a contrast here to the political attitude in the northern cities where the members of the wealthy class, with few exceptions, either remained Tory, and later paid the penalty thereof, or took little active part in the proceedings which led to the birth of our republic!

The architect of the Hammond-Harwood House was one Matthew Buckland whose portrait by Peale served as a frontispiece to the preceding chapter. As yet, we know little about him. Tradition says he was a Philadelphian, but little evidence of that beautiful colonial style of architecture so peculiar to Philadelphia is to be noted in his work here. We do know, however, that he was introduced to one of the Carrolls of Annapolis by George Mason of Gunston Hall.

Possibly no other house in America shows so clearly how our eighteenth-century architects worked. These men took the styles of the old world, adapted them to local conditions, as a rule simplified them in keeping with the simpler background here, and in thus doing evolved a style of their own, which we are justly proud to call American. They rarely slavishly copied the designs which came to them from across the water in the splendid English eighteenth-century books of architecture. They accepted the fundamentals, but generally changed the details according to their own fancies.

Let us throw ourselves back into the period of the designing of the house and imagine ourselves in Buck-

land's office. Charles Willson Peale gave us the atmosphere in the background of his portrait of Buckland. There we see plaster casts, the base of a Doric column, the façade of a Corinthian temple. On the table in front of the sitter are some architectural books, his draughting tools and the completed ground plan of this house. We can be sure that Buckland either owned or had access to those great English elephant folios filled with beautifully engraved plates, whose publication was made possible by advance subscriptions from the nobility and gentlemen of England. Imagine his delight at the receipt of an order which would allow full scope to his learning and imagination. We can see him poring over the pages of that splendid large folio, *A Book of Architecture*, by James Gibbs, London 1728. In *Plate 64* he finds a pedimented house with two wings attached, the general lines of which he believes will meet the requirements of his wealthy client. Here is to be his general scheme. The columnated passageways which attach the wings to the house do not quite meet his approval. They are over ornate. He substitutes for these simple one-story pedimented fronts (page 72), which are much less ornate than the façade of the main portion of the house. In the Gibbs plan, the wings are square and uninteresting. For these Buckland substitutes those beautiful octagonal walls (page 66), so much in vogue in England in the Adam period—a change which emphasizes the classic beauty of the central portion. Buckland evidently was a man who kept himself up to date in architectural styles.

He becomes fascinated by the bull's eye windows in many of Gibbs' pediments. The cartouches interest him. In *Plate 110* he finds a bull's eye window the framing of which certainly is almost the exact prototype of the one used in this house and illustrated on page 71. Here we find the same banded laurel wreath and the same heavy gougings at the side. The shape, in order to fit the opening, needs some adaptation. This he accomplishes by a simplification of the foliage on the sides and a change of certain details of the ornament at top and bottom. Interesting details are the whorls which Mr. Clark's telephoto lens clearly brings out in high relief.* The quoined windows in *Plates 37 and 65* of Gibbs' also catch his eye and probably offer the suggestion for his window (page 80), which lights the stairway.

The doorway of the Hammond-Harwood House

---

*The use of whorls as decorative motives in the backs of Queen Anne chairs of Philadelphia origin can be well studied in a number of chairs of the American wing of the Metropolitan Museum.

(page 65), is justly called the most beautiful colonial doorway in America. The banded laurel below the pediment and of the lintel of the window just over it, and on one mantel (page 103), might well have been taken from illustrations in another of Buckland's books, (we assume he owned them), *The Designs of Inigo Jones* by William Kent, London 1727. From *Plates 56 and 63* Buckland would have been able to obtain the arabesques and peculiar barbaric bird's heads he used in the friezes of the mantelpiece and the doorways in the beautiful dining room he built for Hammond, pages 94 and 86.

One of the books on architecture freely advertised in our colonial news sheets was Abraham Swan's *British Architect*, published in London in 1745. In it we find a drawing of the magnificent cornice which Buckland followed in detail in designing the cornice of the grand dining room, page 92. An interesting feature of Buckland's cornice is the variety of rosettes placed between the modillions.[†] One cannot help but marvel at the elaborately carved inside window shutters (page 86), with their delicate "starfish rosettes" set in alternating octagonal and rounded coffers with carved egg and dart borders.

The carving on the chair rail is equally noteworthy (page 101), as is also the ornamental moulding on the top of the base board, both of which are in thorough keeping with the rich ornament of the mantel, doorways, and doors of this more than remarkable room.

The Adam movement, as we know, gained little foothold in America until after the Revolution. However, in the Hammond-Harwood House, distinct traces of it are to be found. The bead and reel motive used in the door frames is a dominating note in the great work by Robert Adam on *The Ruin of the Palace of the Emperor Diocletian at Spalatro in Dalmatia*, 1764. The gouged motives in the lintel of the door frames may well have been suggested by this beautifully engraved volume, which had such an immediate effect upon English architecture. Other Adam motives which may have been the result of a study of the plates of this monumental volume are the spiral bandings on the dining room door frames and mouldings of the baseboard.

The ballroom above the dining room can certainly be classed as early Adam. The frieze beneath the cornice is composed of a row of Adam vases separated from each other by six beaded channels, page 107. The oval rosettes at the ends of the mantelpiece (page 106), motives often used in the architecture and furniture are of the Adam period; also the bow knots of ribbon from which hang an elaborately carved garland of roses similar to those found in the works of Adam's predecessors.

The interiors of the wings of the house are of great interest. The one on the west was and is the kitchen. It is practically the only restoration in the house.

Among other numerous interesting architectural details in various parts of the house is the placing of a Neptune's trident (page 105), on the keystone arch of the window which lights the hallway.[‡]

It is more than likely that Buckland made his drawing for the mantel (page 103), for the little room off the dining room from some in the book of Inigo Jones, who freely used the paneled block centered between bands of superimposed laurel leaves. To this design, however, Buckland added to the border mouldings in the framing of the fireplace that same bead and reel so often used by the architect of the Temple of Diocletian.

Every visitor to the house is amazed at the furnishings, almost all of which have been provided through the generosity of Mr. and Mrs. Francis P. Garvan of New York, who not only have loaned their choice furniture, but provided the excessively rare old textiles such as were originally in the house.

Color, that dominant note of eighteenth-century interiors, is seen at its best in the pale green walls of the dining room, and in the gray blue walls of the ballroom. On each side of the Peale portrait of Buckland in the dining room hang full length paintings by Wollaston of the Mr. and Mrs. Edmund Jennings who built the beautiful Brice House, another of the treasures belonging to St. John's College.

The Chippendale chairs and Sheraton sideboard belonged to early owners of the house. Much of the furniture is of Maryland origin. All of it shows a high excellence of workmanship and tells the story of the art of the cabinet-maker in America.

The window drapings follow the styles of our early upholsterers. Red and yellow bourettes add great interest to the small rooms on each side of the entrance hall and an eighteenth-century green damask decorates the windows of the small room off the dining room. In the ballroom extraordinary India curtains painted in the beautiful colors of the Orient and in the pattern of the tree of life are reminiscent of the days when the Annapolis newspaper reported the frequent arrival of ships ladened with "European and East Indian merchandise." The toiles de Jouy in the bedrooms with the designs of the "Four Quarters of the Globe" and "America's Homage to France" are of the kind which might well have been sent back to Annapolis by the French officers who enjoyed its hospitality while quartered there during the winter after Yorktown.

Surely St. John's College, the third oldest educational institution in this country, has in this building a great laboratory of American art where students can be given some knowledge of the cultural things of life.

[†]Not having access to the English edition of Swan, I have been obliged to rely upon a copy of the Philadelphia edition which was published the year after the house was completed.

[‡]This interesting detail is found, I am told, in other Maryland tidewater mansions.

Entrance Hall
MATTHIAS HAMMOND HOUSE, ANNAPOLIS, MARYLAND

Grand Dining Room, North Wall

MATTHIAS HAMMOND HOUSE, ANNAPOLIS, MARYLAND

Grand Dining Room, South Wall

MATTHIAS HAMMOND HOUSE, ANNAPOLIS, MARYLAND

Cornice of Dining Room
MATTHIAS HAMMOND HOUSE, ANNAPOLIS, MARYLAND

Dining Room Mantel
MATTHIAS HAMMOND HOUSE, ANNAPOLIS, MARYLAND

Detail of Dining Room Mantel
MATTHIAS HAMMOND HOUSE, ANNAPOLIS, MARYLAND

Front Drawing Room Mantel

MATTHIAS HAMMOND HOUSE, ANNAPOLIS, MARYLAND

Detail of Front Drawing Room Mantel
MATTHIAS HAMMOND HOUSE, ANNAPOLIS, MARYLAND

Detail of Grand Dining Room Door Head
MATTHIAS HAMMOND HOUSE, ANNAPOLIS, MARYLAND

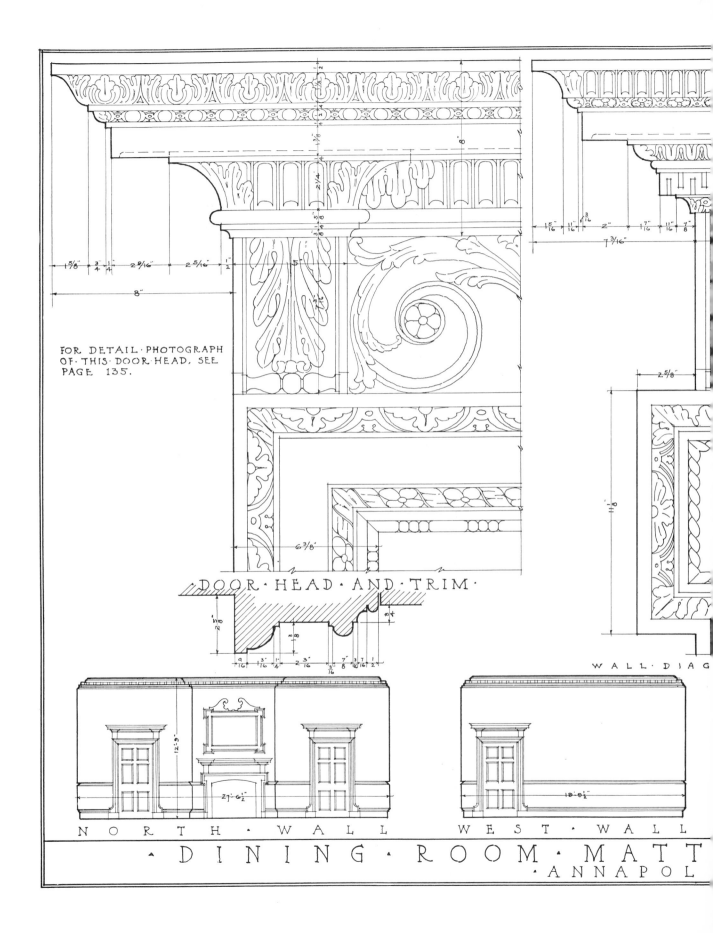

FOR · DETAIL · PHOTOGRAPH
OF · THIS · DOOR · HEAD, SEE
PAGE · 135.

·DOOR·HEAD·AND·TRIM·

·WALL·DIAG

·NORTH·WALL·

·WEST·WALL·

·DINING·ROOM·MATT
·ANNAPOL

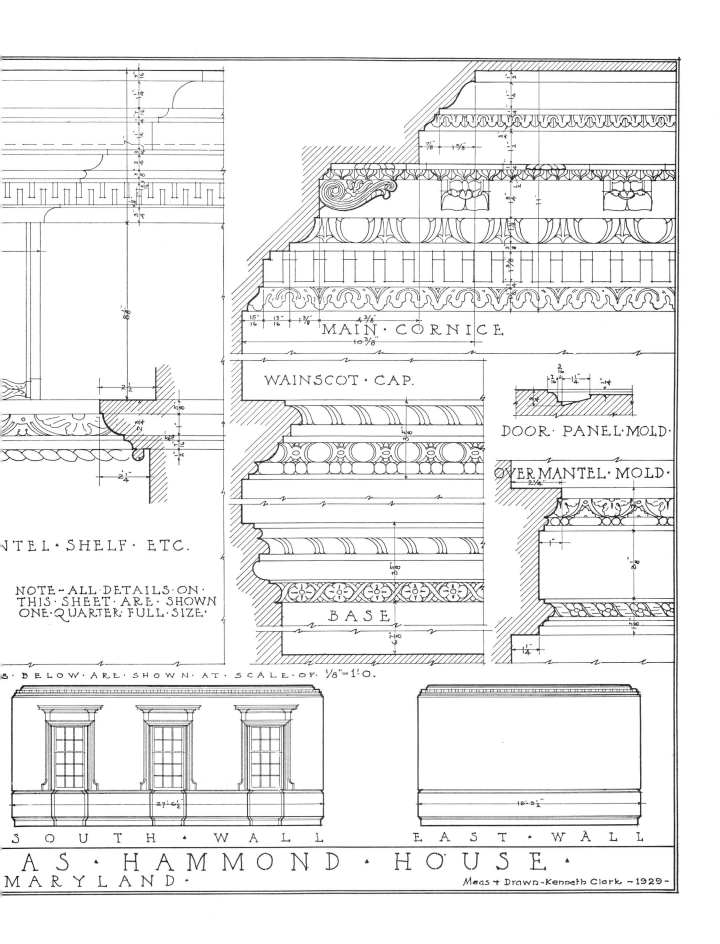

MAIN · CORNICE

WAINSCOT · CAP.

DOOR · PANEL · MOLD

OVER · MANTEL · MOLD

BASE

NTEL · SHELF · ETC.

NOTE - ALL · DETAILS · ON ·
THIS · SHEET · ARE · SHOWN
ONE · QUARTER · FULL · SIZE ·

S · BELOW · ARE · SHOWN · AT · SCALE · OF · ⅛" = 1'·0.

27'-6½"

19'-3½"

S O U T H · W A L L

E A S T · W A L L

A S · H A M M O N D · H O U S E ·

M A R Y L A N D ·

Meas + Drawn - Kenneth Clark - 1929 -

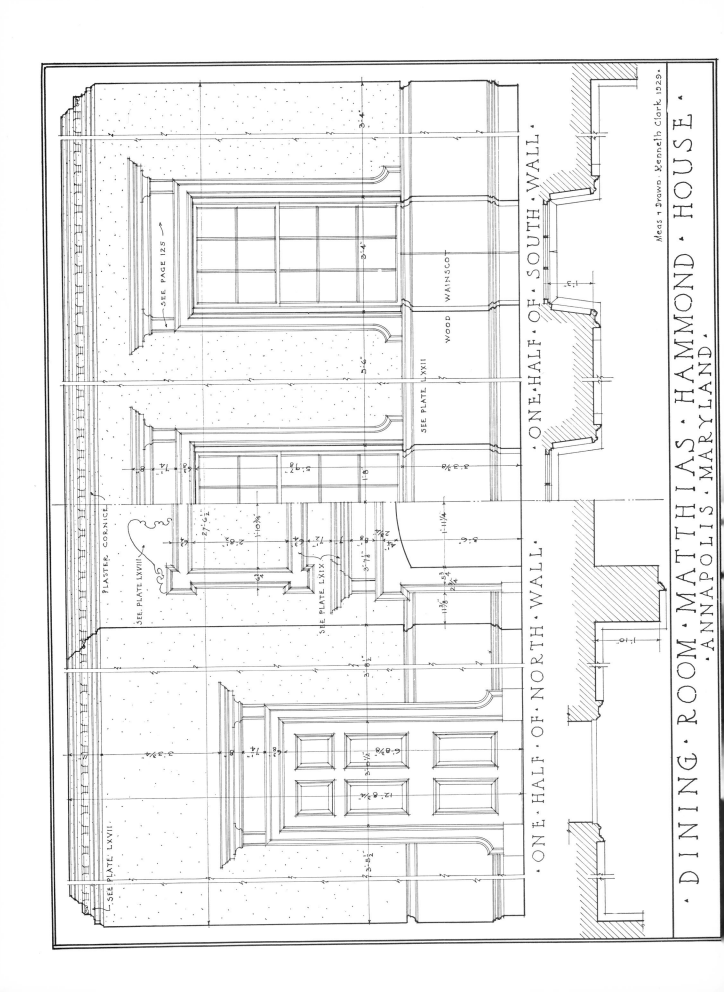

· DINING · ROOM · MATTHIAS · HAMMOND · HOUSE ·

· ANNAPOLIS · MARYLAND ·

· ONE · HALF · OF · SOUTH · WALL ·

· ONE · HALF · OF · NORTH · WALL ·

SEE PAGE 125

WOOD WAINSCOT

SEE PLATE LXXII

PLASTER CORNICE

SEE PLATE LXVIII

SEE PLATE LXIX

SEE PLATE LXVII

Meas + Drawn Kenneth Clark 1929

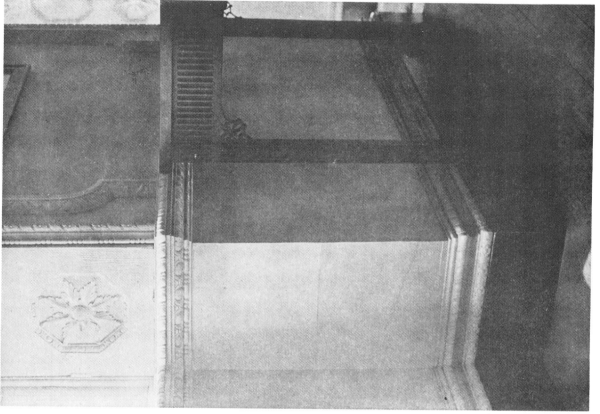

Wainscot and Inside Window Shutter Detail

Mantel Detail
GRAND DINING ROOM — MATTHIAS HAMMOND HOUSE, ANNAPOLIS, MARYLAND

Cornice of Rear Drawing Room
MATTHIAS HAMMOND HOUSE, ANNAPOLIS, MARYLAND

Mantel in Rear Drawing Room
MATTHIAS HAMMOND HOUSE, ANNAPOLIS, MARYLAND

Stair Hall, First Floor
MATTHIAS HAMMOND HOUSE, ANNAPOLIS, MARYLAND

Stair Hall, Second Floor
MATTHIAS HAMMOND HOUSE, ANNAPOLIS, MARYLAND

Ballroom Mantel and Cornice Details
MATTHIAS HAMMOND HOUSE, ANNAPOLIS, MARYLAND

Detail of Ballroom Cornice
MATTHIAS HAMMOND HOUSE, ANNAPOLIS, MARYLAND

Detail of Carved Doorway
MATTHIAS HAMMOND HOUSE, ANNAPOLIS, MARYLAND

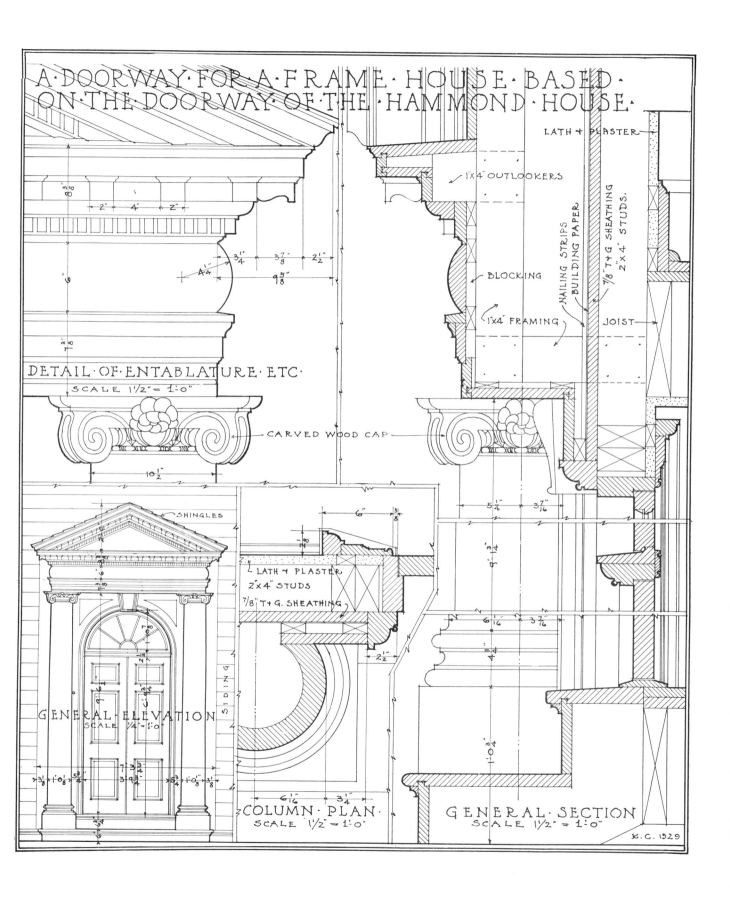

A·DOORWAY·FOR·A·FRAME·HOUSE·BASED· ON·THE·DOORWAY·OF·THE·HAMMOND·HOUSE·

DETAIL·OF·ENTABLATURE·ETC·
SCALE 1½" = 1:0"

LATH + PLASTER

1x4" OUTLOOKERS

BLOCKING

1x4" FRAMING

NAILING STRIPS
BUILDING PAPER

⅞" T+G SHEATHING
2"x4" STUDS.

JOIST

CARVED WOOD CAP

SHINGLES

LATH + PLASTER
2"x4" STUDS
⅞" T+G. SHEATHING

SIDING

GENERAL·ELEVATION
SCALE ¼"= 1:0"

COLUMN·PLAN·
SCALE 1½" = 1:0"

GENERAL·SECTION
SCALE 1½" = 1:0"

K.C. 1929

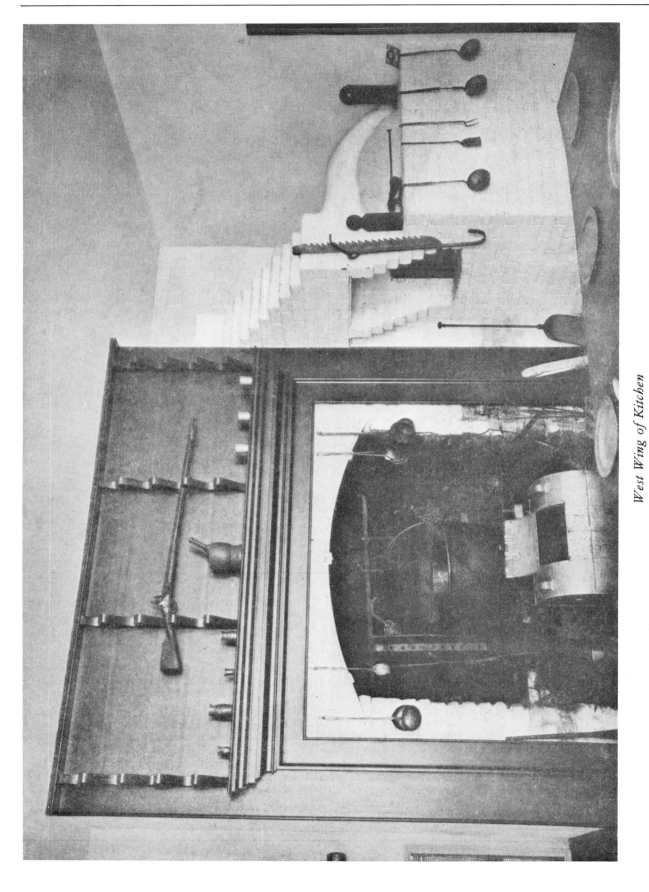

West Wing of Kitchen

MATTHIAS HAMMOND HOUSE, ANNAPOLIS, MARYLAND

The Colonial Renaissance

Text by
Frank E. Wallis
Photographs by
Kenneth Clark
Originally published in 1916 as White Pine Monograph
Volume II, Number 1

Detail of Front Portico

HOMEWOOD—1809—NEAR BALTIMORE, MARYLAND

An example of the second phase of the Southern Georgian. There is an individuality in the planning of these Maryland estates to provide for offices, servants' quarters, tool houses, etc. These were built as story-and-a-half wings, and connected with the main house by one-story corridors. This general scheme was as well adapted to town use as it was to the country house.

THE COLONIAL RENAISSANCE: HOUSES OF THE MIDDLE AND SOUTHERN COLONIES

SINCE the latter days of the eighteenth century, the first indication of architectural sanity was that rejuvenescence or regeneration of the spirit which must have been behind the earlier expressions of architecture in America. Even though we must accept the English Georgian parentage, this Georgian or Colonial happens to be the only style or method which the colonists understood or desired. That this period architecture was interwoven in our fabric of free government, that it housed the conception and completion of our Constitution, and that it formed a stage background for our Fourth of July orations and the perorations of our politicians, must prove to our ultimate satisfaction that Colonial is our national style of architecture.

The renaissance of Colonial happened at the psychological moment, as all the rebirths in architecture have happened; for while the few architects — and they were few, those of the middle nineteenth century — were content and complacent in their fraternal association with the carpenter, there happened to be a small percentage of this baker's dozen of architects who revolted at this immoral association with that "cocotte" of good taste.

Among these few objectors were the original members of the firm of McKim, Mead & White, for I have found records of sketching trips in the late eighteen seventies by Wm. B. Bigelow and by Charles F. McKim; trips made through the old towns of New England, where entire streets of fine examples of the early work had been neglected and undiscovered for more than half a century. There had been a few sporadic attempts to study these examples before this time, but these attempts were confined mostly to the research work of antiquarians and to a few, a sad corporal's guard, of the small number of practising architects.

These two men of the old firm of McKim, Mead & Bigelow had the prior knowledge of the fine examples of Colonial, and, I believe, with few exceptions, were the first architects to succumb to the charms of the old traditions.

It was about this time, too, that Arthur Little of Boston printed a series of pen and ink sketches for private circulation. This book, unfortunately, has disappeared from the ken of man. I remember, however, the great pleasure which the study of this early set of drawings gave me when I began my wanderings in the pleasant land of Colonial architecture.

I was not more than fifteen years of age when the fondness for these old buildings first inspired me, and during the succeeding seven or eight years I measured and made drawings of the old New England work on holidays and after office hours, during which my time was occupied in tracing and designing those illustrious so-called Queen Annes which were actually accepted by architects and laity alike as the supreme expression of good taste in architecture.

The fellows who joined in this quest are to-day scattered throughout the country; indeed, a few of them have mounted *au ciel*. I frequently wonder if Cormer of Seattle, or Charlie Coolidge of Boston, ever remember the rape of the staircase in the old north end of Boston, when we youngsters bribed the complacent tenant to watch for the landlord, and then, with a prepared substitute and a stair-builder, picked out and carried away bodily that beautiful twisted newel post with the varying carved balusters and mahogany rail. "Pop" Chandler, in whose office we installed the stolen trophy, had numerous fits when we informed him that "a kind lady had given the thing to us." The draughtsmen of the office of that time have since become fat and portly architects, such men as Longfellow and Austin, Ion Lewis and dear old Billy Barry, who in himself was a most delightful Colonial expression. His sketches of ships and of old compositions of eighteenth-century buildings were masterpieces; he knew the intimate detail of a dentilled turn in the cornice, the habits of clapboards and rake-mouldings, and the customs and manners of gables and dormers as few other men knew them.

In order to gather sufficient funds for a European trip, it occurred to me that possibly I might acquire such with a few carefully measured drawings of good examples of the Colonial. The plan seemed good and the layouts were not difficult; but I smile today when I remember the rocky path ahead of that unsophisticated youngster who expected to achieve Spain and Italy through the easy by-paths of Colonial drawings.

Ware of the *American Architect* would not even look at the proffered sheets; Col. Meyer of the *Engineering Record* wanted to cut them up, though this big-hearted man tried to sell them for me and offered them to Comstock in New York. This effort was more hopeless than the other with Ware in Boston. Then there comes on the screen that fine old soul whose memory many architects still adore — "Pop" Ware, then in Columbia. These drawings suggested something to him, and his students were permitted to look them over as inspirations for their own summer work. After Prof. Ware

DOUGHOREGAN MANOR, HOWARD COUNTY, MARYLAND

Home of Charles Carroll

had put his seal of approval on these sheets, they were demanded by and sold to the *American Architect*. Today they form a part of *The Georgian Period*.

I have wondered in my later days at the difficulties which I had encountered in disposing of these drawings, realizing, of course, that the profession at that time had little, if any, appreciation of the charm and fitness of that phase which has since come to be known as Old Colonial. I have never been able to comprehend the "Old," though I have been told by one of the grandfathers of the profession that I, myself, was responsible for this false appellation. I wish here to disclaim the credit for the misnomer, and will hereafter, being relieved of this anachronism in phraseology, insist that Colonial is the only correct and proper label for those beauties of the eighteenth century which we today know with such intimacy.

On my return from the European trip I was amazed and delighted to find a representative of Col. Meyer on the dock, a contract in his hand, and with a demand from the virile West that Wallis be looked up and sent South. With this commission and sufficiently financed, I began my journey south, much as Sir Galahad did in his search for the Holy Grail.

I had been face to face with the great expressions of Europe, and had talked with Vedder, with Abbey, and with others in the ateliers of the E. D. B. A. I knew the museums of Madrid, of Florence, of Paris, and of London; the streets and alleys of all of those Spanish, Italian, and French cities where architecture is at home, and where the street gamins and the proletariat are in complete accord with the architectural expressions of their fathers. With the memories of the old world fresh in my mind, and with added experience and knowledge, this Southern trip was much the same to me as those side journeys which I had made into Brittany, Provence, and through the byways and alleys of the architects' paradise.

The Southern journey led to Fells Point in Baltimore, to Annapolis, Fredericksburg, Virginia, Williamsburg, and Yorktown, among others.

I sailed up the York River to Rosewell in a log dugout. How we got there I do not know, but this I remember with pleasure, as I remember the constant courtesy of those Virginia folk, that those at Rosewell permitted me to sketch the beautiful details of that supreme expression in architectural history without any objection.

THE WILLOWS, GLOUCESTER, NEW JERSEY
The walls were built of three-inch planks dovetailed together at the corners. Built about 1720.

I encountered some opposition in Fredericksburg when I essayed so politely to ingratiate myself in the good graces of the *grande dame* who presided as chatelaine over Kenmore, but without success, until the suggestion of the hotel man tempted me to try the husband while the wife was absent. Those of you who read this, coming out of Boston and remembering Dizzy Bridge just about where the Public Library now stands, will chortle with glee when I tell you that because I had been in swimming at Dizzy Bridge I was admitted into the fraternity of old friends by this most charming gentleman. He joined with me in getting results before his wife returned.

It is a fact that archi-

MONTEBELLO — c1812 — NEAR BALTIMORE, MARYLAND
The detail, both exterior and interior, was extremely minute in scale and departed far from classic traditions. This house resembles Homewood both in scale and character of mouldings.

tecture does catch some of the characteristics of those people who create it; the manners and customs of the people, who must necessarily express themselves in brick, wood, and stone and color, must be and are reflected in the buildings. Because of this fact, and because of that other fact that the people of this middle South were more often gentlemen than otherwise—gentlemen not only because of their social assurance, but gentlemen because they were sportsmen in every sense of the word—their architecture shows the reflection; or, rather, their architecture is the physical expression of their own thought and point of view.

There must have been a homey, seignorial atmosphere about the great manor-houses in the heyday of their youth and power that would shame our modern Fifth Avenue magnates, if that were possible. The façades of Westover, Shirley, Brandon, etc., are simple, gentle, and assured, as only the façades of men and women who have assurance of place and family may be gentle and simple. I once saw a thoroughbred girl on the back of a thoroughbred horse, coming up the sward from the James to a thoroughbred house—that of Carter's Grove: a perfect picture and a most natural conclusion, for the house was in the class with both Diana and the horse. And these other types might be, and indeed must be, accepted as the progeny of the more stately and dignified châteaux of the great landowners of colonial times, for here we find the same completeness, the same constraint against over-adornment.

The streets in the little villages of the South are lined with these charming and restful homes, and you will also find in the type which we will call the outhouses of the great mansions, the same care in design and the same restraint in composition and ornament which are illustrated in the charming Williamsburg, Falmouth, and Fredericksburg examples: all of them supreme in their place, and all of them creating a restful atmosphere such as you may find between the covers of *Cranford*.

Have you read *Cranford*? If you have, you may possibly appreciate the charming ladies at Harwood House, Annapolis. If you know this classic, the story of the flower garden, the dinner to which these charming ladies invited the *wanderlust* youngster, the sweet appreciation of his quest, will appeal to you, even though you have not been invited to church service, as I was invited—invited to join them in their old high-back pew.

Was George Washington a finer and broader man because of his life at Mount Vernon, or was Mount Vernon and its type, such as we know them, beautiful because of the desires of those old worthies who cussed and smoked and tippled, meanwhile fighting our battles and planning our independence from George of England?

We may find Georgian examples through the shires of England. Cork has some of them; Dublin also, and London is colored with its expression. Georgian, however, and not Colonial, for our Colonial, the son of the Georgian, if you please, has clapboards, porches in Doric and Corinthian or near Corinthian, cornices and modillions, or cornices ornamented with the invention of our own native joiners; for wood to these old men was a servant, and they played in and out through the grain of the woods for their curves and their applied ornaments in such fashion as would have shocked the stolid Britishers of the Georgian times.

The drawings and sketches made of the Southern work suggested a book on the subject, and I was again commissioned to go South, although this first book—and I believe it was the first book published on the Colonial—included sketches made in New England, etc. Those other books of photographs and drawings which followed this publication have added tremendously to our knowledge of Colonial, and in the later days the fellows who, like Deane, Bragdon, Chandler, Brown, Embury, and Bessell, have studied the varying phases and who have written books and articles on the subject, have placed the country under great obligations, for these publications have served their part in the development of good taste in architecture.

Editor's Note: The identification of the house at the top of page 119 as the Peyton Randolph House is incorrect. The photograph was taken in 1916 before the restoration of Colonial Williamsburg began. Subsequent research revealed that the house belonged to James Semple, a judge and professor of law at the College of William and Mary. It is also known as the William Finnie residence, in honor of one of its early colonial occupants.

TUCKAHOE — c1707 — GOOCHLAND COUNTY, VIRGINIA

The scene of Thomas Jefferson's boyhood. It is the oldest of the James River frame mansions. The house reveals an interesting plan which is ⊥ in shape: the library, drawing room and stair hall in one wing, with the ballroom connecting the rear wing, in which the dining room, bedroom and second stair hall are located.

TEDINGTON — 1717 — SANDY POINT, CHARLES CITY COUNTY, VIRGINIA.

Named after a place in London. The house has massive walls of brick and from the first floor is weather-boarded over the inside brick casing; known in colonial days as a "stock" building, and supposed to be indestructible. The estate is on the James River.

AN EARLY COTTAGE, FALMOUTH, VIRGINIA
Long dormers with sharp-peaked gables are characteristic of the early Southern houses.

TUCKER HOUSE, WILLIAMSBURG, VIRGINIA
The houses in this section followed the same general plan, the various departments located in ells or extensions clustered in a rambling manner about the central building. This house, like a majority of the Southern colonial houses, has a bedroom on the ground floor. The windows are glazed with small panes set in lead.

HOUSE OF PEYTON RANDOLPH, WILLIAMSBURG, VIRGINIA
Mr. Randolph was the first President of the Continental Congress.

HOUSE ON DUKE OF GLOUCESTER STREET, WILLIAMSBURG, VIRGINIA
Williamsburg was founded in 1632. It was the center of colonial growth in the
South from 1698, when Governor Nicholson removed the seat of government from
Jamestown to this place. The town contains many excellent examples of low,
picturesque wooden houses built in the latter part of the seventeenth century.

RISING SUN TAVERN, FREDERICKSBURG, VIRGINIA

There is a beautiful hall and stairway. All bedrooms have slanting ceilings. Washington slept at this place when he came to visit his mother.

MARY WASHINGTON HOUSE, FREDERICKSBURG, VIRGINIA

There are many interesting old houses in Fredericksburg, among them the frame cottage in which Mary the mother of Washington lived and where she died.

MOUNT VERNON MANSION, FAIRFAX COUNTY, VIRGINIA
Probably the most notable of Virginia plantations, the home of George Washington.

WYE HOUSE — c1780 — TALBOT COUNTY, MARYLAND
The original manor-house was built in 1662. A fragment of this is now used as an outbuilding. The main building contains the principal rooms and connects by corridors with one-story wings in which are the library on one side and the domestic offices on the other. The whole façade is two hundred feet in length.

THE GLIBE, POWHATAN COURT, VIRGINIA

An example of the use of a large central dormer with smaller ones
on either side; characteristic of houses of this class in the South.

DR. BILDERBECK'S HOUSE — 1813 — SALEM, NEW JERSEY

The bead-edged clapboard walls are painted yellow and the trim is white. There has been an unfortunate
twentieth-century excrescence added at the side. The building is otherwise intact and as sound as when first built.

GOVERNOR EDEN HOUSE — c1750 — EDENTON, NORTH CAROLINA
The framed overhang construction is most unusual in the Southern colonies.

PENDELTON HOUSE, NEAR RICHMOND, VIRGINIA
The early Virginia colonists built their houses of wood. A characteristic feature of these early houses was the chimney at each end built outside the house wall for its entire height. The occurrence of the gambrel is not nearly so frequent as in the North, and there are few examples of framing with the overhang.

Springhouse and Dairy

ESTATE OF GOODLOE HARPER — c1800 — BALTIMORE COUNTY, MARYLAND

Houses of this type were built near a spring or cold, swift-running brook. There is a sunken trench all around inside the outside wall about 18 inches deep and 18 inches wide. The cold water enters at one side of the house and goes out the opposite side. The water is regulated by a gate so that it will not rise beyond the height of the milk jars, which are set in the trenches.

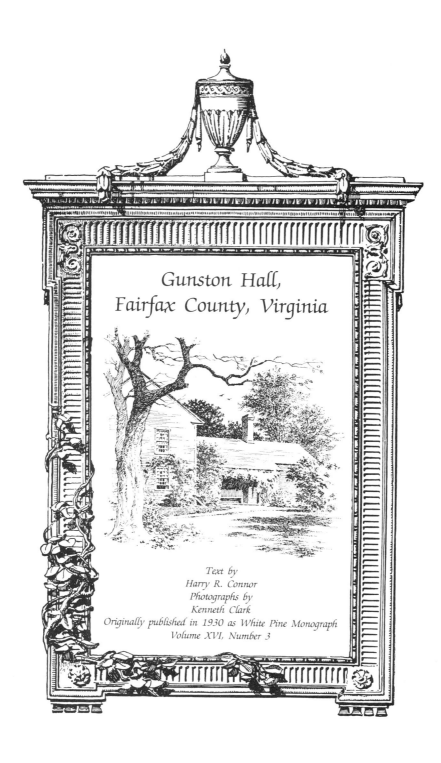

Gunston Hall,
Fairfax County, Virginia

Text by
Harry R. Connor
Photographs by
Kenneth Clark
Originally published in 1930 as White Pine Monograph
Volume XVI, Number 3

Southern Façade of Porch
GUNSTON HALL, FAIRFAX COUNTY, VIRGINIA

GUNSTON HALL, VIRGINIA

GUNSTON Hall has a familiar and pleasant old world sound and indeed the first "Hall" to bear that name was in Brewood Parish in old Staffordshire, England, in the hamlet called Gunston. George Mason, the Revolutionary patriot, named his Potomac plantation mansion house for that ancestral seat.

There was a George Mason of the Virginia Company in 1620 who may have been the father of the Cavalier, Col. George Mason—the great-grandfather of George Mason of Gunston—who embarked for America sometime about 1651 and took up grants of land in Westmoreland, the country extending northward "to the falls of the great river Pawtomake" above what is now Georgetown, District of Columbia. The Cavalier increased his land holdings in 1664 and in 1669 and held the office of County-Lieutenant of Stafford, an office conferred on the class of "gentlemen" or large landholders. The second and the third George Mason added to the large estates of the family which at one time comprised seven thousand acres.

The fourth George Mason, builder of Gunston Hall, was born in 1725. At twenty-five, he married Anne Eilbeck and in 1758 occupied his newly completed mansion—the stately seat of a gentleman of family and culture—in the region with other landed gentry living at Mount Vernon, Belvoir, Stratford and Chantilly. These places were the social centers of that section of the colonies and their masters maintained a certain state.

George Washington, although seven years younger than George Mason, was a neighbor and a boyhood friend. The private journal of Washington contains many records of his intimacy with Mason. They attended races and balls together, went to hunts and vestry meetings and spent days surveying the bounds of their contiguous lands. Mount Vernon Mansion is on a point only five miles up the river from Gunston Hall but is sixteen miles by road.

When it is considered that the builder of Gunston Hall was called by Jefferson "the wisest man of his generation" and was to Madison the "ablest debator" and to those who have studied his life "a genial, well-read, cultivated gentleman and a man of social parts," it is not difficult to understand that he could not be satisfied with any house which, in respect of design, of material and of finish, was not correct and refined.

The influence of Sir William Chambers, English architect (1726–1796), is perceptible in many of the homes of the Virginia tobacco and wheat planters. No doubt, George Mason was familiar with the works erected and treatises published by Chambers in England, and perhaps used them as a guide and inspiration in the design of his home. We know that Chambers shares the honors with Chippendale of adapting Chinese forms to decorative furniture and that he adhered to the Anglo-Palladian traditions during the Greek Revival in England. The treatment of the southeast room with its "Chippendale" character may well have been inspired from one of Chambers books.

It is not our mission here to surmise, but to set down notes which may give a hint of the manner of man who built Gunston Hall and point out a few of the facts which are not evident in the photographs and measured drawings.

Gunston Hall is situated on a height on the right bank of the Potomac River about a half mile from the shore and the southern front commands a full view of the river. From the portico on this front, one descends directly by a long narrow walk, bordered by box, through an extensive garden. The box was said by Lord Balfour of England to be the finest he had ever seen. The house is about three miles from the highway and a private road leads up to the northern front. Here is a portico of four small columns with an arch, forming a Palladian motif. The exposures are actually northwest by west and southeast by east.

We have an extract from an unfinished manuscript of Gen. John Mason, a son of the builder of Gunston Hall, published in Kate Mason Rowland's *Life of George Mason* which enumerates the dependencies erected in connection with the mansion. The manuscript reads, "To the west of the main building were, first, the school house, and then a little distance, masked by a row of large English walnut trees, were the stables. To the east was a high paled yard, adjoining the house, into which opened an outer door from the private front, within or connected with which yard were the kitchen, well, poultry houses and other domestic arrangements; and beyond it on the same side were the corn house and granary, servants' houses (negro quarters), hay yard and cattle pens, all of which were masked by rows of large cherry and mulberry trees." We are indebted to this

record of the original outbuildings, for the only surviving evidence is the stone well-curb.

Gunston Hall was erected in the adapted Georgian
style. It suffered some defacements after it passed out
of the hands of the Mason family. The house was restored some time ago, however, under the direction of
Glenn Brown, architect, and is now the valued possession of Mr. Louis Hertle who makes it his permanent
residence and to whom the publishers are indebted for
the privilege of recording it in this series.

The plan of the house is the most common of Colonial
types — four rooms to a floor with a transverse stair hall.
The hall is spacious and is of a width in proportion to
the total depth and is perfectly symmetrical although
the stair rises along one wall and lands on the other so
that the interior spaces are unbalanced. The southeast
room, the drawing room, is the most elaborate and has
been selected for the subject of the measured drawings
on pages 138 and 139. The principal floor plan is shown
on page 130, but we have not shown the arrangement
of space in the high cellar with windows above ground
which extends under the entire building. Here were the
wine vaults in which was stored the old Madeira, the
favorite imported wine of the early Virginian.

The rooms on the second floor open on each side of a
hall which runs at right angles to the hall below and
terminates at each gable end of the house. These rooms
are small and low-pitched with dormer windows and
wide low window seats. A steep ladder leads up from
the hall into the attic. This upper region is lighted and
ventilated by a round window in each gable end of the
house. The walls are made of large red brick laid up
in Flemish bond. The angles of the walls are emphasized
by raised blocks or quoins of cut stone. This treatment
is a characteristic of the late Renaissance in England.
The walls are terminated with well designed cornices
of wood, which on the end elevations become large
coves, and are painted white in conjunction with the
window frames to give pleasant contrast to the façades.

The window openings are notably tall in proportion,
about 2½ to 1. Mullions and transoms had gone out of
general use about this time in England and sash windows
were introduced. In Gunston Hall, the sash windows
are placed almost flush with the outer face of the walls.

The roof pitch is higher than is usual in examples of
the Georgian style, but this fact has been grossly exaggerated in the sketches and drawings which have ap-
peared in print heretofor. The elevation shown on page
130 is accurate and makes other drawings appear dis-
torted and misleading. Dormer windows take the place
of the windows in the gables of the Jacobean period and
so we find the second floor rooms lighted by ten dormer

windows placed over the windows and openings of the
first story.

As usual, tradition and gossip have attributed the
fine wood carving and mouldings of the interior of
Gunston Hall to "convict craftsmen from England,"
to actual "importation of the finished products from
England," etc. We do not know the name of the wood-
worker, but we feel sure that he was not left to his
own devices in the execution of the design, for the
details are too well studied in relation to the proportion of each room and each opening in each room, to
have been left to the workman or ordered from "stock"
from across the sea. The door enframement with pilasters
was unusual before the Revolution — there are examples
in Charleston, South Carolina, and Maryland, but
they all date after 1758. Gunston Hall has, also, a
most elaborate window treatment, internally; a pair of
pilasters with full entablature. The employment of open
semicircular niches, a variant of the semicircular door
head, is first found in American domestic architecture
in this house. It was the woodworkers and the carpenters
who gave the decorative accessories of Colonial houses
their chief distinction.

Of all the seats on the Potomac River, Gunston Hall
is the most well studied adaptation of the English Georgian style and presents a splendid picture of a tidewater Virginia house. Although only a story and a half
high, and simple in design, it was evidently the work of
one who knew and valued the virtues of proportion and
dignity and delicacy of detail. Here as usual architectural merit can not vie with historical interest and Gunston Hall will always be known and venerated for being
the scene of some of those early expressions of colonial
disaffection which finally led to the War of the Revolution. George Mason will always be remembered as the
author of the Bill of Rights and the Constitution of Virginia, and for his intimate association with the Declaration of Independence. We feel that, to his other cultural
accomplishments, including the design of the State Seal
of Virginia, credit should be bestowed upon Mason of
Gunston for his share in the production of his important
house. He died at home in 1792 and is buried on the
property, as was the custom in his day.

Gunston Hall is one of the eighteenth-century country
mansions of the South still standing as a symbol of a
life which was on a grand scale for the few — made possible by the slavery of the many. "There are said to have
been five hundred persons on the estate, including the
several quarters." — *Life of George Mason.* An excess of
cheap labor over a long period usually results in the
blossoming of a high culture and here that result is
exemplified.

Garden Façade

GUNSTON HALL, FAIRFAX COUNTY, VIRGINIA

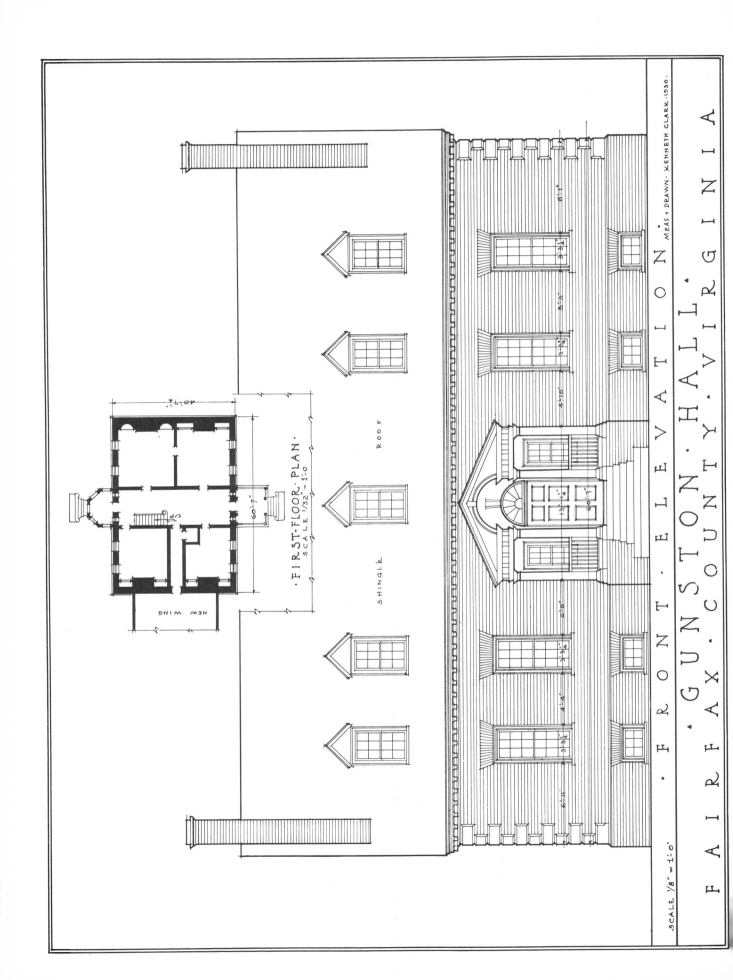

·FIRST·FLOOR·PLAN·
SCALE 1/32"=1'·0

NEW WING

ROOF

SHINGLE

SCALE 1/8" = 1'·0'

· F R O N T · E L E V A T I O N · MEAS'D DRAWN' KENNETH CLARK·1930.

· G U N S T O N · H A L L ·

F A I R F A X · C O U N T Y · V I R G I N I A

GUNSTON HALL, FAIRFAX COUNTY, VIRGINIA

Cornice Detail
GUNSTON HALL, FAIRFAX COUNTY, VIRGINIA

Porch Detail, Northern Façade

GUNSTON HALL, FAIRFAX COUNTY, VIRGINIA

Staircase Detail
GUNSTON HALL, FAIRFAX COUNTY, VIRGINIA

Hall
GUNSTON HALL, FAIRFAX COUNTY, VIRGINIA

Library
GUNSTON HALL, FAIRFAX COUNTY, VIRGINIA

Drawing Room Window Detail
GUNSTON HALL, FAIRFAX COUNTY, VIRGINIA

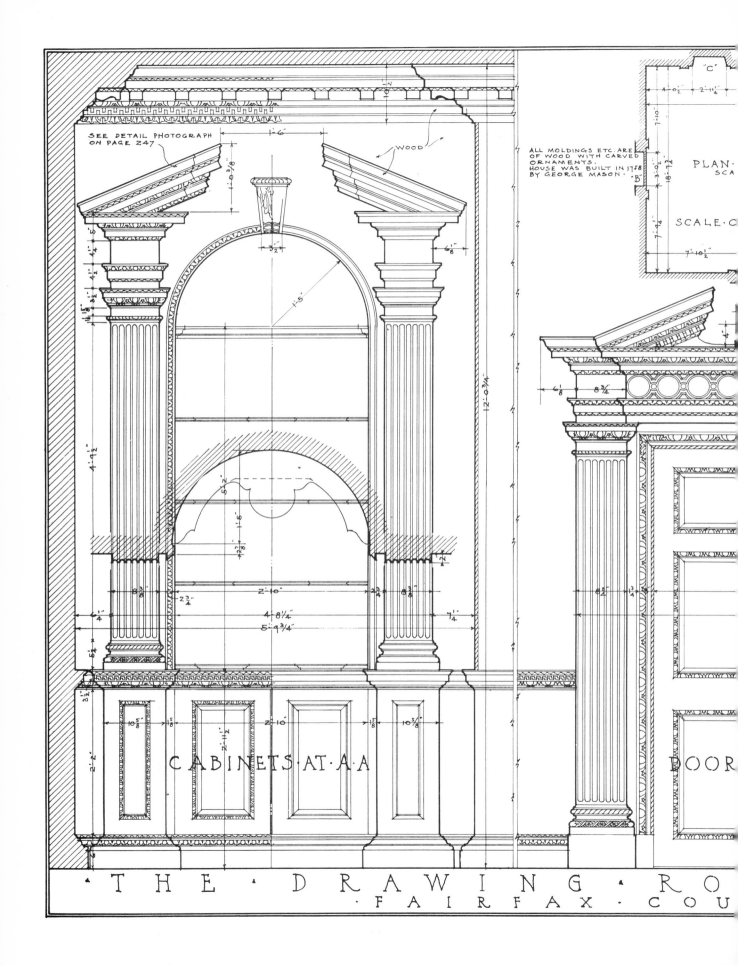

SEE DETAIL PHOTOGRAPH
ON PAGE 247

WOOD

ALL MOLDINGS ETC. ARE
OF WOOD WITH CARVED
ORNAMENTS.
HOUSE WAS BUILT IN 1758
BY GEORGE MASON.

PLAN·

SCA

SCALE·O

CABINETS·AT·A·A

DOOR

·THE· DRAWING · R O
·FAIRFAX· C O U

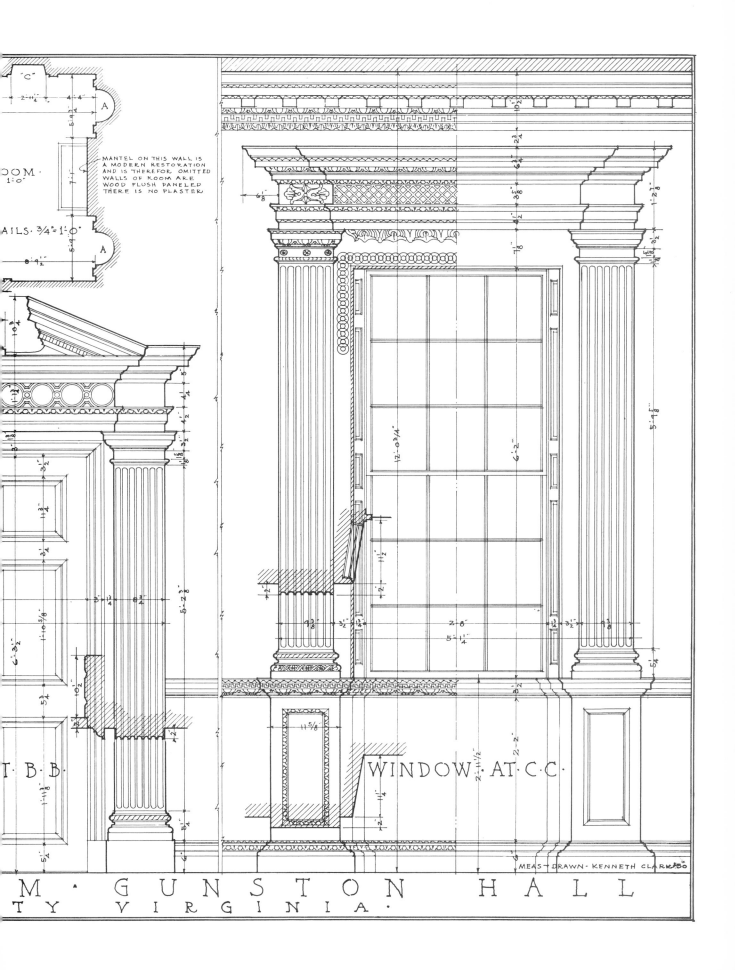

MANTEL ON THIS WALL IS
A MODERN RESTORATION
AND IS THEREFOR OMITTED
WALLS OF ROOM ARE
WOOD FLUSH PANELED
THERE IS NO PLASTER

WINDOW · AT · C · C ·

MEAS · DRAWN · KENNETH CLARK '30

M · GUNSTON HALL

TY VIRGINIA ·

STUCCO   WOOD

STONE

· DETAIL · OF · FRONT · PORCH ·

SCALE 3/8" = 1'-0"

MEAS & DRAWN – KENNETH CLARK '30

· GUNSTON · HALL ·
· FAIRFAX · COUNTY · VIRGINIA ·

Drawing Room Doorway
GUNSTON HALL, FAIRFAX COUNTY, VIRGINIA

Drawing Room Doorway Detail
GUNSTON HALL, FAIRFAX COUNTY, VIRGINIA

Drawing Room Wainscot Detail
GUNSTON HALL, FAIRFAX COUNTY, VIRGINIA

Drawing Room Cabinet and Cornice
GUNSTON HALL, FAIRFAX COUNTY, VIRGINIA

Drawing Room Window Detail
GUNSTON HALL, FAIRFAX COUNTY, VIRGINIA

Chippendale Room
GUNSTON HALL, FAIRFAX COUNTY, VIRGINIA

Garden Façade
GUNSTON HALL, FAIRFAX COUNTY, VIRGINIA

Detail of Northern Porch
GUNSTON HALL, FAIRFAX COUNTY, VIRGINIA

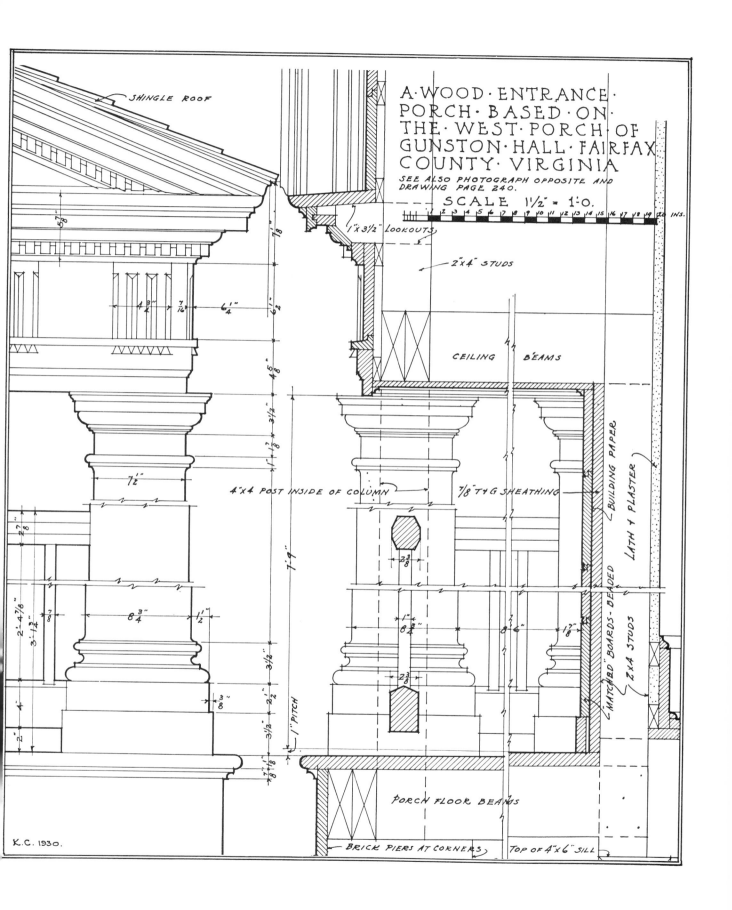

SHINGLE ROOF

A·WOOD·ENTRANCE·
PORCH·BASED·ON·
THE·WEST·PORCH·OF
GUNSTON·HALL·FAIRFAX
COUNTY·VIRGINIA
SEE ALSO PHOTOGRAPH OPPOSITE AND
DRAWING PAGE 240.
SCALE 1½" = 1'0.

1' x 3½" LOOKOUTS

2" x 4" STUDS

CEILING BEAMS

BUILDING PAPER

LATH & PLASTER

4" x 4" POST INSIDE OF COLUMN

7/8" T & G SHEATHING

MATCHED BOARDS - BEADED

2 x 4 STUDS

1" PITCH

PORCH FLOOR BEAMS

K.C. 1930.

BRICK PIERS AT CORNERS

TOP OF 4" x 6" SILL

House Viewed From the Garden
GUNSTON HALL, FAIRFAX COUNTY, VIRGINIA

Some Charleston Mansions

Text by
Joseph Everett Chandler
Photographs by
Kenneth Clark
Originally published in 1928 as White Pine Monograph
Volume XIV, Number 4

MILES BREWTON HOUSE, 27 KING STREET, CHARLESTON, SOUTH CAROLINA

SOME CHARLESTON MANSIONS

IF there is one quality which more than any other seems to run like a beneficial alloy through all our Colonial architecture it is its distinct friendliness—its human scale and hominess. One sees this most convincingly in the minimum house of the early followers of husbandry in New England, and as one proceeds further south through the Middle Atlantic states and the scale and elegance of the early habitations increase, there seems no diminution of this fortunate quality.

Still further south in the softer climes where easily obtainable labor made living more leisurely, and the scale of the house increases commensurately, one might expect greater severity of social intercourse; but always there seems to remain that atmosphere of hospitable companionship. In the city of Charleston, South Carolina, one pauses before one of the most grandiose of early Colonial residences in a not notably important street (except that it is named King Street) and finds its portico almost on the sidewalk line, but separated from it by iron gates and a spiked whorl above the fence which is so extreme in its violent convolutions as to remind one of the barking dog which has no bite, and to produce more a feeling of amusement than any other at the extreme battle array. So still the feeling is one of friendliness and it is probable that the placing of the mansion in close proximity to the street operates here, as in New England, to dispel any feeling of aloofness. In fact it is rarely that we find large grounds and gardens in connection with any village or urban example of this subtle type of architecture—even the examples in the country being placed as a usual thing inconspicuously. Only when we encounter the mansions of Philadelphia in Fairmount Park, and our two most notable examples of spacious surrounding grounds—Mt. Vernon, and Westover on the James River—do we find park-like proportions in the setting of the houses, and then nothing commensurate, say, with The Priory just out of Bath, England and many, many others there of Georgian type. In our two examples, the river is but a short distance from the house and the nearness in each case bespeaks ease of intercourse and friendliness.

This Miles Brewton Mansion (opposite) often called the Pringle House, is one of the few very early houses which has survived several disastrous fires in the city, but it was antedated by a similar one built by Honorable Charles Pinckney.

Although placed so near the street line there is ample garden space in the rear. The large gateposts flanking the entrance to the stable court on one side of the house form an impressive feature which one finds constantly recurring throughout the city—a comparatively small house frequently having this lordly feature. And several times one sees, as here, a glimpse of the stable playfully designed as "something different" with a primitive form of Gothic window opening and a half gable, reminiscent of Tudor England. Here, on page 155, is a glimpse of another feature which astounds northerners, the Spanish type of tiled roof, until one recalls the constant early intercourse with the West Indies, close by, and realizes that the frequent fires of the city made imperative a fireproof roofing. Many examples of this type of roofing existed until recent years in Charleston and in the immediate past they have been still further depleted.

Most fittingly, however, is this type of roof still preserved on the Old Powder Magazine—originally a picturesque part of a Bastion of the City Wall and the only early building remaining in Charleston which of a surety was built in the seventeenth century.

The interior details of the Brewton-Sawter House here shown exhibit a rather curious divergence from the more usual type around Charleston—something recalling mantels further north around New York, where the fanlike spandril form in the upper corners of the frieze was used quite commonly as well as the radiating lines of the oval in the center panel. The identical use of the wainscot cap throughout the lower part of the entablature of the mantel which is simplified by this substitution for the pilaster cap is not exactly unusual, but being attractively enriched calls special attention to the feature and seems to tie the mantel proper into the general finish of the room. This "entablature" of most mantels is so free in its departure from strictly classical proportions in its relation of cornice to exaggerated frieze and suppressed architrave—in this instance like the wainscot cap—that it hardly warrants the nomenclature, except that early English examples such as those of Gibbs and Milton—which abide by classic divisions more closely, have fixed the tradition. Other details of this room are hardly as happy, such as the great width and multiplicity of mouldings in the architraves surrounding the windows; the awkward way in which the cornice of the room begins by a plump ovolo suggesting that the true beginning of the cornice may have been covered by the plaster of the ceiling; the shapeless brackets and the profusion of mouldings immediately above the dentil course as well as immediately below it. Then too, there is the detrimental use of a frieze of striking ornament further made noticeable by the use of rosettes — those circular whorls which easily become too prominent if of much size.

The custom in most of the Charleston houses of note of placing the main floor of the house over a basement entirely above ground offered a great opportunity for that distinction which invariably comes from well designed steps. Often the drawing room was on the second floor above the basement offering an opportunity for elongated proportions in the upper stories resulting in added dignity of effect. The Miles Brewton House has the first floor placed much lower than most of the notable houses as this custom seems to have been a gradual growth perhaps resulting through frequent communication with the West Indies, causing the builders to gradually elevate the important stories. This feature together with the tiled roof, offers two points of departure from the usual Colonial architecture of the rest of the states and makes the work of this city and its surrounding towns and plantation houses distinct.

A simple rendering of this feature is shown in the two houses built by Daniel Blake in Court House Square with an arched entrance at the sidewalk level, making a common service entrance for both, while the main entrances are at a considerably higher level and reached by attractive steps and landing.

The admirable Bull-Blacklock House, 18 Bull Street, built in 1800 is a splendid example of the treatment of this feature while the impressiveness of the large carriage entrance gates and posts places the architectural value of the house well up among the mansions of the town. Here again we see the use of wooden gates both for the carriage entrance and the more intimate service entrance of the house, the latter being enriched to a point which apparently shows a substitution of wood for iron either as a matter of economy or the inability to get iron work of the character which is indicative of the city.

The characteristic type of Charleston house belonging to this city alone, and finally arrived at through climatic requirements and manner of living, is seen in considerable statliness in the Henry Manigault House at 18 Meeting Street, is here shown on page 160. The long living room frontage is toward the garden and the narrow end of the house on the street, with entrance door in a prolongation of the first floor street façade, the door bell of which reaches distant regions in the service ell and invariably results in a long wait for the caller, and finally audible footsteps the length of the long piazza.

On page 172, we see as in the City Park wall, the fascinating arched reveals, the proper planting of which makes a delightful background for a garden.

To the already great variety of types of houses in the architectural ensemble of this remarkable city — influenced as it was by the direct English strain — that of the French Huguenot influx in the latter part of the seventeenth century; with the slight touches of the doughty Dutch from Nova-Belgia and the quiescent Quaker, and still further by the Spanish influence from the West Indies — there is added a strikingly northern note — even of New England — in the charming house — page 166 — built by one Nathaniel Russell (a name from the heart of New England) distinctly different from all the others except that it adapts one major and unique Charlestonian feature, and even here seen only semi-occasionally — that of the many sided bay. In this case it is, if memory serves, a half elongated octagon on the exterior, its farthest projection being the point of an angle and becoming a circular room within by a padding of its interior angles. Of this remarkable feature there is another fine example still extant in the Middleton House and a legend exists of another one on the East Battery which was destroyed. This surprising and thoroughly delightful feature being treated in splendid scale in both the Russell and Middleton houses has a most satisfying charm. From the delicate balustrade of the roof down through the well proportioned cornice, the perfection of window lintels, and well proportioned key-blocked arches to the iron balconies of a detail common to New England in design, but here adopting a local variation in a beautiful shape which bows out in the center of each window on the street façade — all is satisfaction. The form of the belt-course between the second and third stories seems the only divergence from the New England type, and the circular caps of iron bolts somewhat interrupting the belt course attest a comparatively recent addition of iron rods through the building necessitated by the unfortunate racking of earthquake tremors.

The fence alone is the sole disappointing feature in this beautiful and distinct piece of architecture, it apparently being either a comparatively recent substitution or may indicate a sudden disaster to Charleston architecture by the death or removal of the remarkable artisan who did such wonderful work in the way of embellishing the gates and balconies of this beautiful city.

Iron Entrance Gate, Fence and Stable
MILES BREWTON HOUSE, 27 KING STREET, CHARLESTON, SOUTH CAROLINA

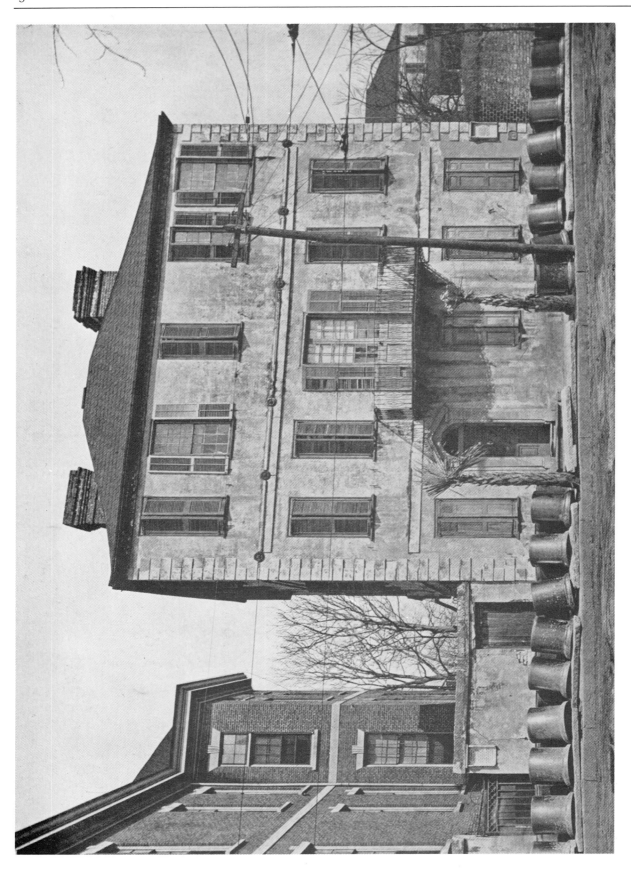

RALPH IZARD HOUSE—BEFORE 1757—110 BROAD STREET, CHARLESTON, SOUTH CAROLINA

WILLIAM BLACKLOCK HOUSE—c1800—18 BULL STREET, CHARLESTON, SOUTH CAROLINA

WILLIAM BLACKLOCK HOUSE, 18 BULL STREET, CHARLESTON, SOUTH CAROLINA

DANIEL BLAKE HOUSES—1760–1772—COURT HOUSE SQUARE, CHARLESTON, SOUTH CAROLINA

HENRY MANIGAULT HOUSE, 18 MEETING STREET, CHARLESTON, SOUTH CAROLINA

Detail of Mantel in Second Floor Drawing Room

BREWTON-SAWTER HOUSE, CORNER OF CHURCH AND TRADD STREETS, CHARLESTON, SOUTH CAROLINA

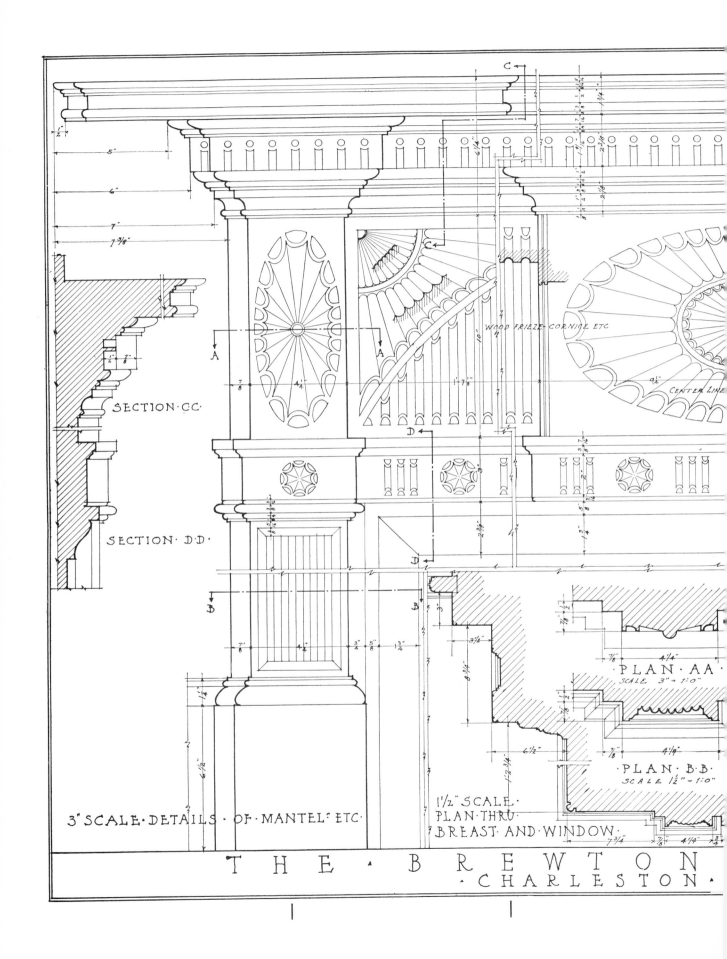

SECTION·CC·

SECTION·DD·

WOOD·FRIEZE·CORNICE·ETC

CENTER·LINE

PLAN·AA·
SCALE 3" = 1'·0"

PLAN·B·B·
SCALE 1½" = 1'·0"

3"·SCALE·DETAILS·OF·MANTEL·ETC·

1½"·SCALE·
PLAN·THRU·
BREAST·AND·WINDOW·

THE·BREWTON

·CHARLESTON·

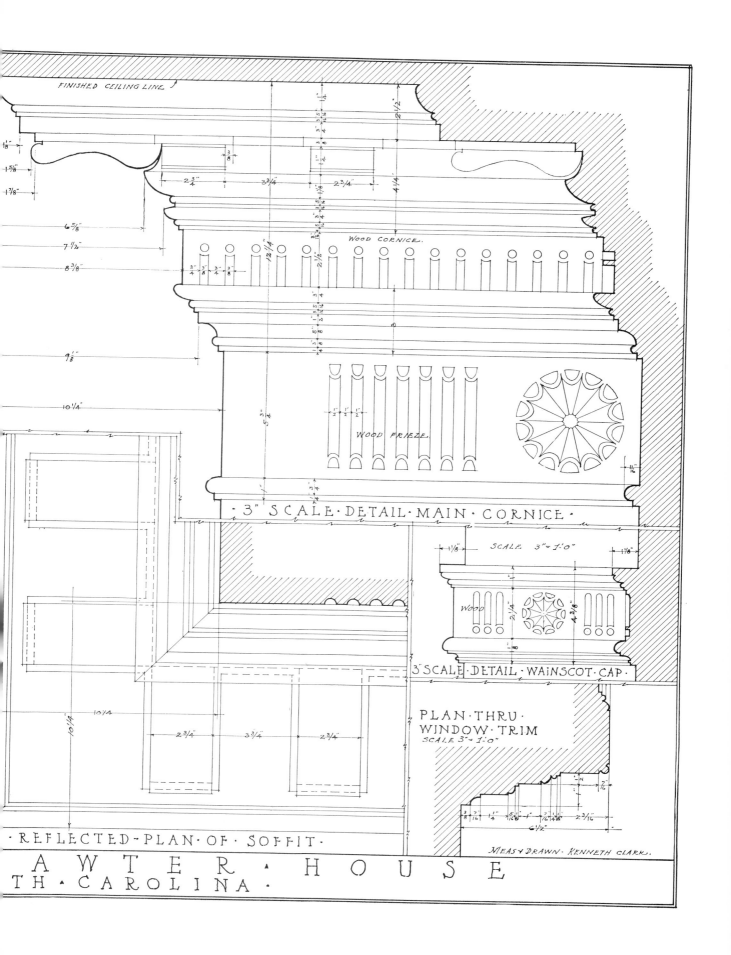

FINISHED CEILING LINE

WOOD CORNICE.

WOOD FRIEZE.

· 3" · SCALE · DETAIL · MAIN · CORNICE ·

SCALE 3"= 1'-0"

WOOD

· 3" SCALE · DETAIL · WAINSCOT · CAP ·

PLAN · THRU ·
WINDOW · TRIM
SCALE 3"= 1'-0"

· REFLECTED · PLAN · OF · SOFFIT ·

MEAS & DRAWN · KENNETH CLARK.

A W T E R · H O U S E
TH · CAROLINA ·

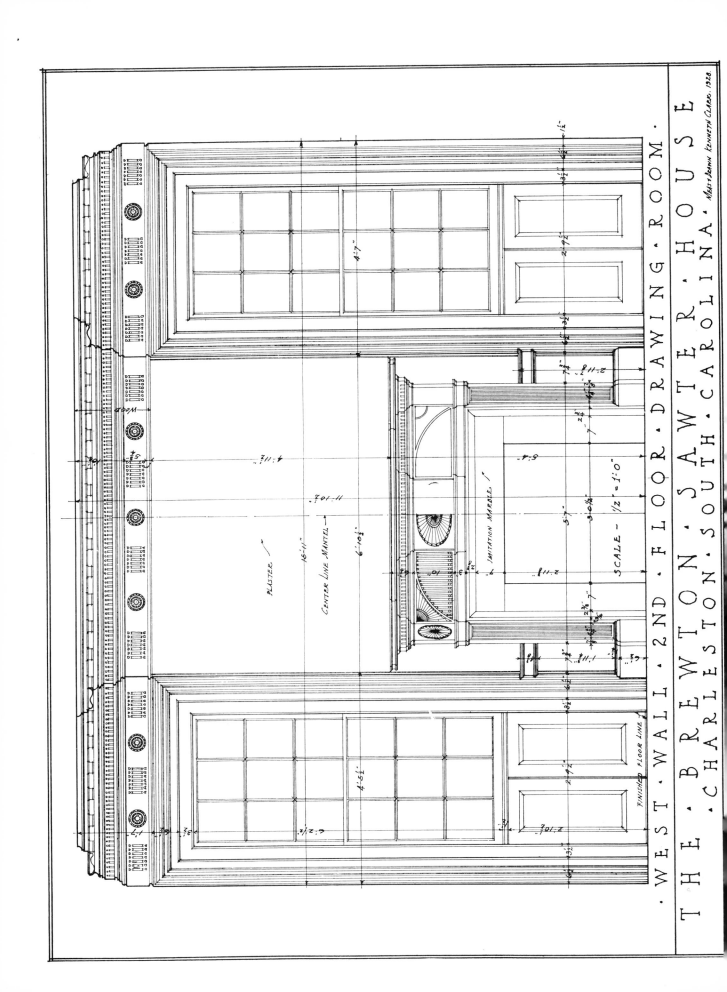

· W E S T · W A L L · 2ND · F L O O R · D R A W I N G · R O O M ·

T H E · B R E W T O N · S A W T E R · H O U S E

· C H A R L E S T O N · S O U T H · C A R O L I N A · MEAST·DRAWN KENNETH CLARK·1928·

SCALE - 1/2" = 1'·0"

PLASTER

CENTER LINE MANTEL

IMITATION MARBLE

FINISHED FLOOR LINE

Second Floor Drawing Room West Wall

BREWTON-SAWTER HOUSE, CHURCH AND TRADD STREETS, CHARLESTON, SOUTH CAROLINA

NATHANIEL RUSSELL HOUSE—BEFORE 1811—51 MEETING STREET, CHARLESTON

DANIEL BLAKE HOUSES—1760–1772—COURT HOUSE SQUARE, CHARLESTON, SOUTH CAROLINA

HOUSES AT 25 AND 27 MEETING STREET, CHARLESTON, SOUTH CAROLINA

HOUSE AT 35 MEETING STREET, CHARLESTON, SOUTH CAROLINA

Double-Hung Window With Doors
BREWTON-SAWTER HOUSE, CHARLESTON, SOUTH CAROLINA

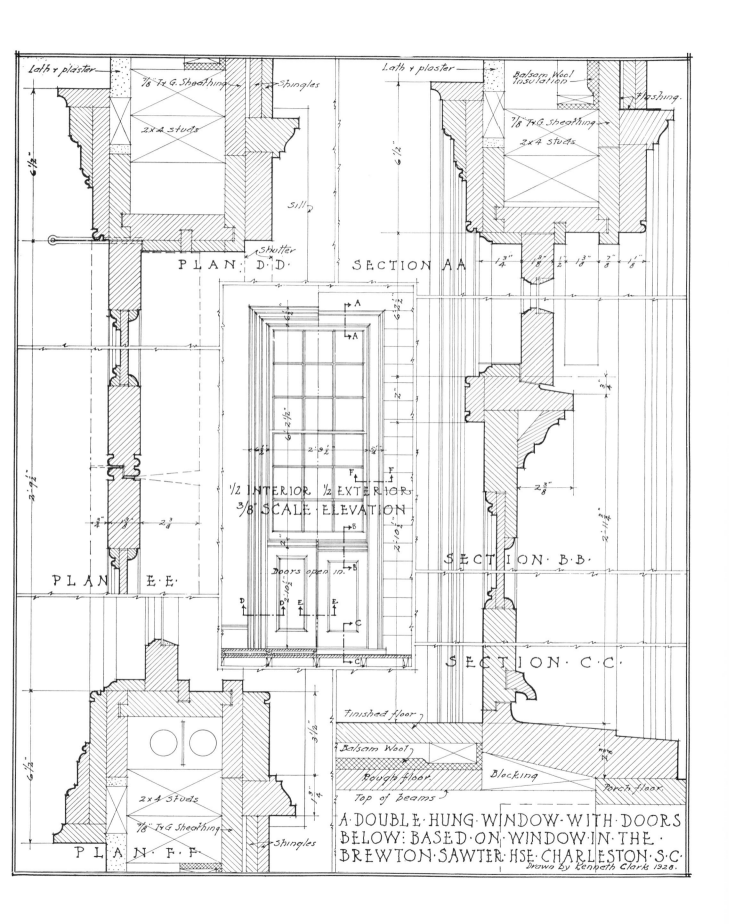

Lath + plaster

⅞ T+G. Sheathing · Shingles

2×4 studs

PLAN·D·D·

6½"

Sill

Shutter

Lath + plaster

Balsam Wool Insulation

Flashing.

⅞ T+G. Sheathing

2×4 studs

6½"

SECTION·A·A·

1¾" 1⅞" ½" 1⅛" ⅞" 1⅛"

A
A

PLAN·E·E·

2'-9½"

¾" 1⅝" 2⅜"

6'-2½"

½ INTERIOR ½ EXTERIOR
⅜"·SCALE·ELEVATION

2'

6'-2½"

SECTION·B·B·

3"
4

2⅜"

2'-11¼"

F   F

B
B

2'-10½"

Doors open in.

D   D
N
E   E

C
C

SECTION·C·C·

3½"

1¾"

Finished floor

Balsam Wool

Rough floor

Blocking

Porch floor.

Top of beams

1¾"

PLAN·F·F·

2×4 studs

⅞ T+G. Sheathing

Shingles

6½"

·A·DOUBLE·HUNG·WINDOW·WITH·DOORS·
BELOW·BASED·ON·WINDOW·IN·THE·
BREWTON·SAWTER·HSE·CHARLESTON·S·C·

Drawn by Kenneth Clark 1928.

HOUSE AT 301 EAST BAY, SOUTH, CHARLESTON, SOUTH CAROLINA
Built about 1800.

Smallwood-Jones Residence, New Bern, North Carolina

Text by
Kenneth Clark
Photographs by
Kenneth Clark
Originally published in 1927 as White Pine Monograph
Volume XIII, Number 3

SMALLWOOD-JONES HOUSE, NEW BERN, NORTH CAROLINA

AN EASTERN NORTH CAROLINA TOWN HOUSE: THE SMALLWOOD-JONES RESIDENCE

THE merchant prince of today parades the arrogance of his fortunes before the world, by building a palace; a thing of magnificence, housing the treasures for which the world has been combed—Old Masters, statuary, tapestries and all the priceless *objets de vertu* available at the time his agents were endowed with the usual *carte blanche* commission to purchase.

When all is done, his friends and the public "Oh!" "Ah!", admire and envy and there has been created another museum. The architect has earned another trip to Europe and the decorator a fleet of Rolls-Royces. The one thing lacking in the finished masterpiece is *HOME!* The idea of creating something in which a family can be born, grow up and die, is not part of the picture.

No one can imagine the happy group gathered before the Louis XIV mantel, seated in comfort on the delicate gold legged and *petit point* backed chairs, with Mother knitting and Father deep in the evening paper, while the children play on the Kermansha museum piece until it is time to go to bed. Hardly! Mother and Father are in Europe, different parts of Europe, perhaps. The son is spoofing the professors at Yale or Harvard, while the daughter is wearing out her $40 slippers and her constitution at some night club. The house, the people and the age are attuned, and the tune is "She's My Baby" not "Home Sweet Home."

Could anything be in greater contrast physically and spiritually to the homes of the Colonial period and of the Early Republic? The rich men of that day, allowing for the change in values and the comparative amounts called fortunes, were privileged to pick and choose as to their house and its contents just as they are today. The resulting houses, that have survived, are a monument to the taste and the sense of the fitness of things of our forefathers. These old houses radiate the warmth of feeling that inspired their conception and bespeak in a quiet, dignified, yet powerful voice the qualities and characteristics which went into the making of the American nation. They reflect the home-loving natures

and appreciation of the beautiful that these sturdy farmers and merchants possessed before the U.S. of our country was combined to make a dollar sign on which the eagle could perch and scream his financial defiance to the world.

The Smallwood-Jones House at New Bern, North Carolina, is a survival of a prosperous period in the early days of that community. Built by an architect and a builder of whom research does not reveal the names, it is an excellent example of what the well-to-do merchant of that place and time considered to be the proper thing for himself and family. It is a small house, the entire original building being enclosed with a space of 36 x 40 feet, but the interior gives an impression of spaciousness and stateliness which belie the actual dimensions. Facing on East Front Street, with its rear overlooking a long grassy vista sloping to the banks of the River Nuse, it has seen the coming and passing of many generations, and survived the vicissitudes of fire, flood and war. It has been tenderly cared for through succeeding generations and is today in the hands of sympathetic and appreciative people who are restoring it and placing it in condition to survive the coming years, that posterity may see, admire and reflect.

The front elevation presents to the street a simple, reserved aspect with components beautifully spaced in a richly textured wall of common brick. The bonding is Flemish and the brick joints, of gray mortar, are about ⅜ of an inch wide and struck flush with the surface. Both brick and mortar have weathered until they have reached the point which gives these old brick walls the quality that accounts for much of their charm; so difficult to reproduce in new work. The spacing of openings is symmetrical except for the dormers which do not center over the windows below. The main cornice, the porch and the dormer pediments are lavishly decorated with hand-carved ornament. Because New England has always been extolled as the source of nicely executed detail, etc., while the South has been considered as lacking the proper craftsmen, it is hard to realize that the ornamental work on the Smallwood-Jones House was done locally. However, there is every reason to believe that the carving was done here and it ranks with the best of the old work irrespective of time and place.

The detail, moulding systems and other individual parts of the cornices, etc., are decidedly original in design and placing and, where most of the New England detail can be assigned to a definite inspirational source, such as Langly, Paine, or other authorities of the period, this work has an originality and freshness that is individual to it and the similar houses of this town. There is a very indefinitely founded tradition in New Bern that these houses were done by one James Coor, a naval architect or builder of ships who came there in 1800 to practice his profession and turned his talents to architecture. Such a tradition might account for some of the unorthodox detail, which, with the use of the rope moulding so consistently, has a decidedly "shippy" look.

The ugly block which terminates the porch capitols shown on page 181 is a modern repair, the originals being similar to the pilaster caps shown on page 180. The roof was originally shingled, but was replaced at a later day by one of the less sympathetic standing seam tin. With the exception of the few changes mentioned, the exterior presents its original appearance.

The plan is unusual in that it has a hall 11' 2" wide at the right side running through the house with a door in the rear wall and another at the side. This seems at first glance an uneconomical feature, but in reality this hall forms a second living room, well ventilated from three exposures, and in the warm summer must be a comfortable and practical room. To the left of this hall as one enters is the room known as the counting room which a former owner set aside as an office and which was at one time entered direct from the street by the cutting down of the left-hand window of the elevation to form a door; this was probably done long after the house was built and it has since been filled in and the elevation restored to its original appearance. The counting room has a fine mantel to which has been added an over-mantel treatment that does not agree in scale with the original. Back of the counting room and also opening off the hall at the right, is the dining room, with a gem of a mantel and wainscot and a cornice that caps the room with a real feeling of scale (see page 194). The relation in size of the cornice and its members to those of the over-mantel cornice and the pediment just below is a remarkable example of judgment of scale on the part of the designer meriting serious consideration, for were one or the other too large or too small by the smallest amount the scale of the entire room would suffer. The relation is, however, perfect and contributes in no small measure to the "handsomeness" and dignity of the whole. The service to the dining room was originally from the basement, which accounts in part for the modern addition of kitchen, pantry, etc., at the rear.

The second floor is unique in that it has the formal drawing room necessitated by the use of the usual first floor space for the counting room. In this second floor drawing room, we see the genius of the architect and the skill of his craftsmen, who executed the work, at their best. Here was lavished all they knew of decoration in its architectural sense. All the old gagets, dentils, ropes, frets, wave motives, interlacement bands and carved sunbursts are here, but all are used in their proper place, so well designed and scaled that each goes to make up the ensemble without intruding its individuality. The ornament is of carved wood, the work of a master craftsman; the rope mouldings are cut in the round and applied; the fret and the interlacement band are jig-sawed out of 3/16" stuff and nailed on with hand-made nails, of which there is hardly an evidence on the surface. The paneling has the moulds cut on the stiles and the panel set in solid without a back mould. All is dovetailed and dowelled together in the manner of the ancient cabinet-maker who had the time and the inclination to do things right, once, and for all time. There is a new door in this room which was added to the east wall in modern times and though the workmen tried to copy the old work exactly the *"Touch"* is not there. Even on close examination, it is difficult to point out any apparent variation, but the whole thing has a different look. The craftsman has been succeeded by the mechanic, the artist by the plane pusher.

To the east of the drawing room is a small room, perhaps originally a library, with the same trim and embellishments as the former. There is some evidence that this was at one time part of the drawing room, making one long room entirely across the front of the house, but it seems hard to account for this in plan if the window on the east elevation which has been moved, was formerly on axis.

The entire house, inside and out, shows a careful, studied solution of a domestic architectural problem that the modern architect may study with profit. As an inspiration in designing a modern American house, it is certainly more fitting than the Italian, Spanish and other foreign styles that have been "the thing" lately. American architecture has an indigenous background that deserves more consideration at the hands of her architects than it is given. If the young American, whose steps are on the brink of an architectural career, would take heed to the slogan "See America First," our homes would begin to reflect our ancestry and not the "Melting Pot."

SMALLWOOD-JONES HOUSE, NEW BERN, NORTH CAROLINA

Side Porch
SMALLWOOD-JONES HOUSE, NEW BERN, NORTH CAROLINA

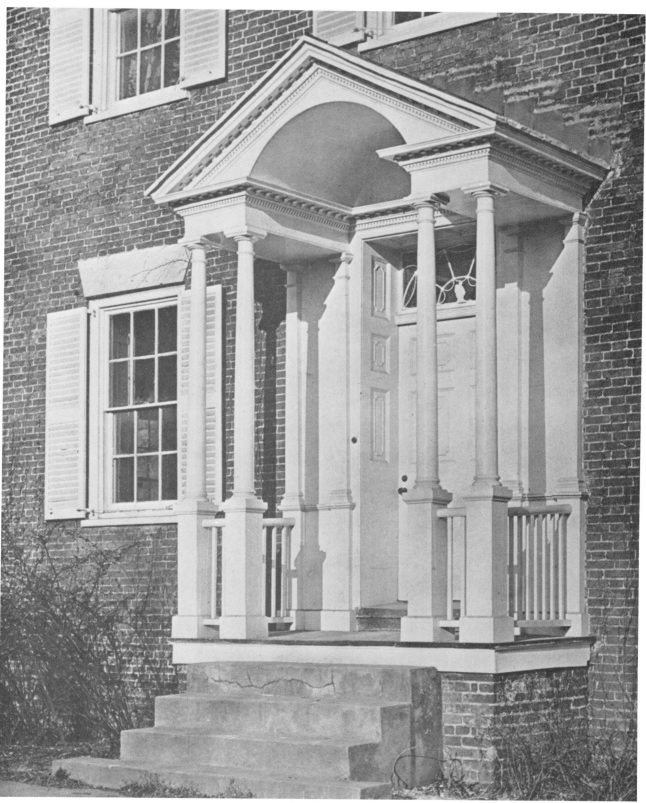

Front Porch
SMALLWOOD-JONES HOUSE, NEW BERN, NORTH CAROLINA

Detail of Front Porch
SMALLWOOD-JONES HOUSE, NEW BERN, NORTH CAROLINA

Detail of Front Porch
SMALLWOOD-JONES HOUSE, NEW BERN, NORTH CAROLINA

Detail of Window
SMALLWOOD-JONES HOUSE, NEW BERN, NORTH CAROLINA

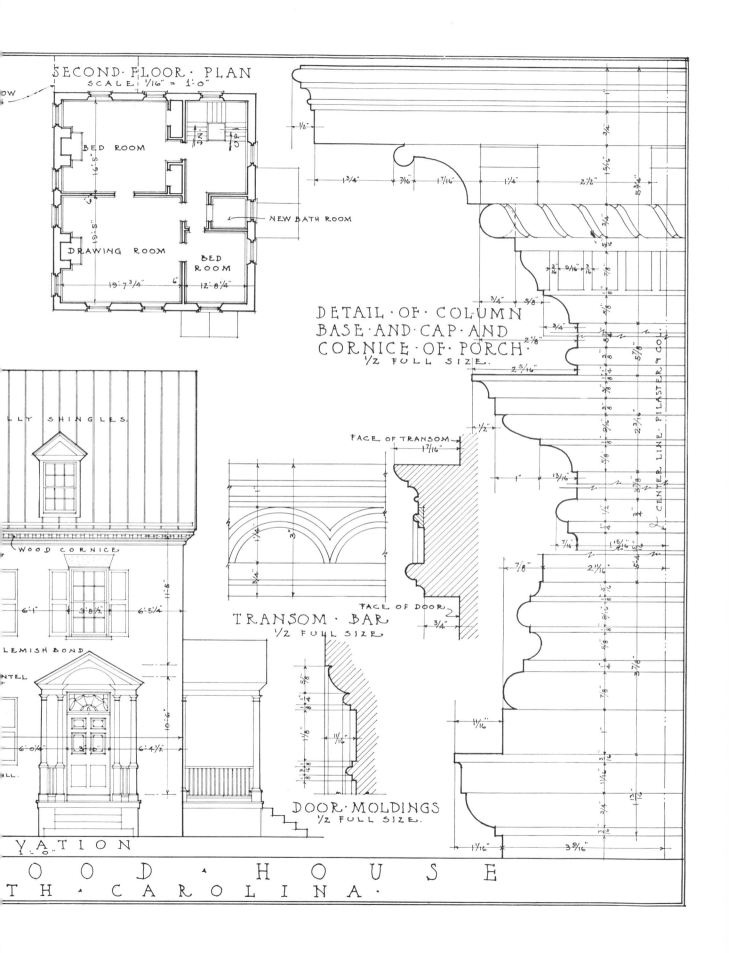

SECOND · FLOOR · PLAN
SCALE: 1/16" = 1'-0"

BED ROOM

16'-5"

DRAWING ROOM

BED ROOM

NEW BATH ROOM

19'-7 3/4"   12'-8 1/4"

DETAIL · OF · COLUMN
BASE · AND · CAP · AND
CORNICE · OF · PORCH ·
1/2 FULL SIZE.

CENTER · LINE · PILASTER & COL.

SHINGLES.

WOOD · CORNICE

FLEMISH BOND

6'-1"   3'-8 1/2"   6'-5 1/4"

FACE OF TRANSOM
1 7/16"

FACE OF DOOR

TRANSOM · BAR
1/2 FULL SIZE

6'-0 1/4"   6'-4 1/2"

DOOR · MOLDINGS
1/2 FULL SIZE.

YATION

OOD · HOUSE

TH · CAROLINA ·

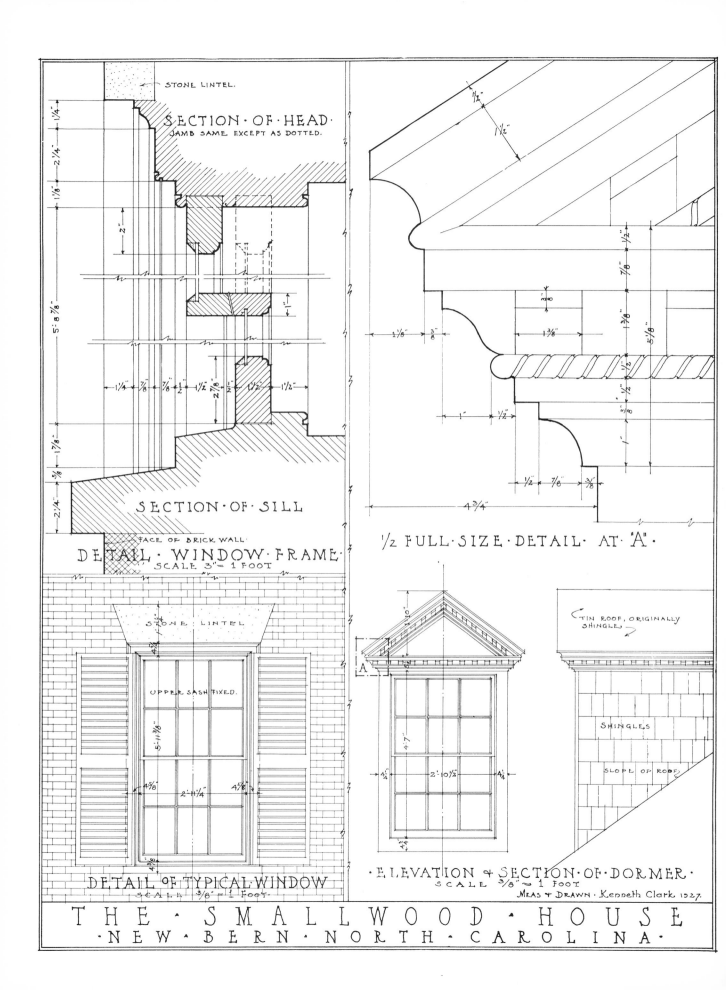

STONE LINTEL.

SECTION · OF · HEAD ·
JAMB SAME EXCEPT AS DOTTED.

SECTION · OF · SILL

FACE OF BRICK WALL

DETAIL · WINDOW · FRAME
SCALE 3" = 1 FOOT

½ FULL · SIZE · DETAIL · AT · "A" ·

STONE · LINTEL

UPPER SASH FIXED.

DETAIL OF TYPICAL WINDOW
SCALE 3/8" = 1 FOOT.

TIN ROOF, ORIGINALLY SHINGLE

SHINGLES

SLOPE OF ROOF

· ELEVATION & SECTION · OF · DORMER ·
SCALE 3/8" = 1 FOOT
MEAS & DRAWN · Kenneth Clark 1927.

THE · SMALLWOOD · HOUSE
· NEW · BERN · NORTH · CAROLINA ·

Detail of Dormer and Cornice
SMALLWOOD-JONES HOUSE, NEW BERN, NORTH CAROLINA

Second Floor Drawing Room

SMALLWOOD-JONES HOUSE, NEW BERN, NORTH CAROLINA

For measured drawings of this room, see Volume II, Chapter 9.

First Floor Hall

SMALLWOOD-JONES HOUSE, NEW BERN, NORTH CAROLINA

For measured drawing of this stair, see Volume II, Chapter 9.

Detail at Foot of Stairs
SMALLWOOD-JONES HOUSE, NEW BERN, NORTH CAROLINA

Stair at Second Floor Level
SMALLWOOD-JONES HOUSE, NEW BERN, NORTH CAROLINA

Cornice
SMALLWOOD-JONES HOUSE, NEW BERN, NORTH CAROLINA

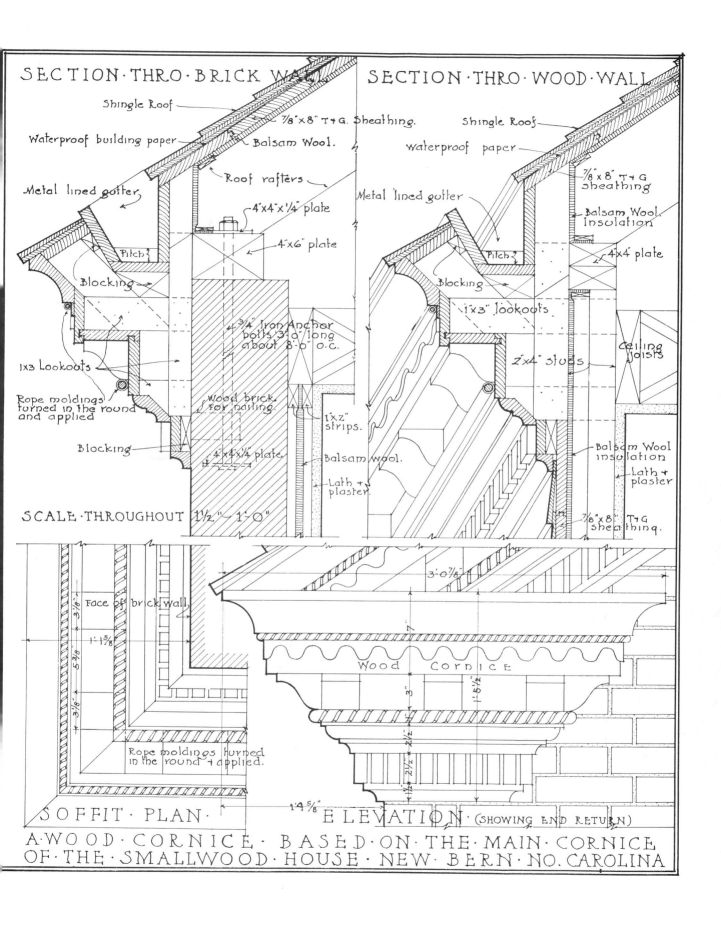

SECTION·THRO·BRICK·WALL

Shingle Roof

Waterproof building paper

Metal lined gutter

Pitch

Blocking

1x3 Lookouts

Rope moldings turned in the round and applied

Blocking

⅞"×8" T+G. Sheathing.

Balsam Wool.

Roof rafters

4"×4"×¼" plate

4"×6" plate

¾" Iron Anchor bolts 3'-0" long about 8'-0" O.C.

Wood brick for nailing.

1"×2" strips.

Balsam wool.

Lath + plaster.

4"×4"×¼" plate

SECTION·THRO·WOOD·WALL

Shingle Roof

Waterproof paper

Metal lined gutter

Pitch

Blocking

1×3 Lookouts

2×4 studs

Ceiling joists

⅞"×8" T+G sheathing

Balsam Wool Insulation

4×4 plate

Balsam Wool insulation

Lath + plaster

⅞"×8" T+G sheathing

SCALE·THROUGHOUT 1½" = 1'-0"

Face of brick wall

3⅜"

1'-1⅝"

5⅞"

3⅜"

Rope moldings turned in the round + applied.

SOFFIT·PLAN·

3'-0⅞"

Wood Cornice

3"

1'-5½"

2½"

2½"

2½"

2½"

1½"

1'-9⅝"

ELEVATION· (SHOWING END RETURN)

A·WOOD·CORNICE·BASED·ON·THE·MAIN·CORNICE·OF·THE·SMALLWOOD·HOUSE·NEW·BERN·NO. CAROLINA

Detail of Dining Room Mantel
SMALLWOOD-JONES HOUSE, NEW BERN, NORTH CAROLINA

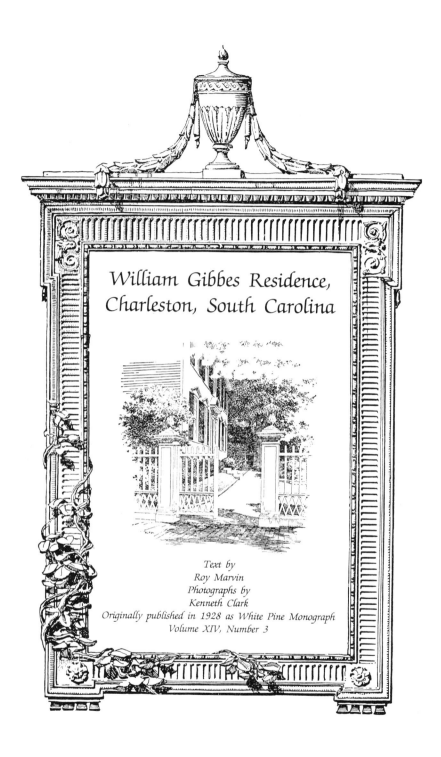

William Gibbes Residence, Charleston, South Carolina

Text by
Roy Marvin
Photographs by
Kenneth Clark
Originally published in 1928 as White Pine Monograph
Volume XIV, Number 3

Detail of Façade
WILLIAM GIBBES HOUSE, 64 SOUTH BAY STREET, CHARLESTON, SOUTH CAROLINA

A TOWN HOUSE OF CHARLESTON, SOUTH CAROLINA: THE WILLIAM GIBBES RESIDENCE

WHEN Josiah Quincy of Massachusetts visited Charleston in 1773, he was impressed by the material prosperity and hospitality of the people in the Carolina colony. In his published diary he wrote: "This town makes a beautiful appearance as you come up to it and in many respects a magnificent one. I can only say in general that in grandeur, splendor of buildings, decoration, equipages, numbers, commerce, shipping and indeed everything, it far surpasses all I ever saw, or can ever expect to see in America."

Charleston was isolated from its neighbors and the other sections of America. Dense forests separated the town from the other English colonies and there were Indians on the west and Spaniards to the south. Commerce with the northern colonies was obstructed by the perils of the voyage around Cape Hatteras. These facts together with the character of the early settlers tended to make them independent in thought and action. One has a feeling that this independence exists even today. Surely a civilization and a sophistication have been created which are comparable to the most aristocratic of capitals. Charleston is the last remaining American city in which Madeira and Port and *noblesse oblige* are fully appreciated and exercised according to the finest traditions.

Just before Josiah Quincy's visit, four prominent citizens of Charleston, Robert MacKenzie, Edward Blake, George Kincaid and William Gibbes undertook to reclaim the salt marsh lands to the south of South Bay Street. It is interesting to note that even with the unlimited acreage of land available during the earliest days of colonization that a large part of the town is built on land reclaimed from the shores of the sea and rivers. The settlers were evidently intent upon making Charleston one of the few seaports in the world where a direct view of the ocean might be had from the city.

The walled in and filled up South Bay Street section was practically completed by 1772 and the reclaimed

land was conveyed to Samuel Legaré and later to William Gibbes. The records show that both Gibbes and Blake built houses on the land included in this second conveyance soon after it came into Gibbes possession.

William Gibbes came direct to America from England. He took a prominent part in the life of Charleston and was active in behalf of the colonies until the actual beginning of the hostilities with England. With native Americans living in London, he petitioned the King in favor of the colonies and then at the opening of the Revolution escaped to Bermuda, and thence home.

The residence which is the subject of this chapter is supposed to have been built by William Gibbes sometime before 1776. The records would seem to confirm this belief. The land on which the house now stands belonged to Gibbes and five years after his death in 1789 this house was sold to Mrs. Sarah Smithe for a consideration of £2500.

The ground floor or the basement of the Gibbes House is entered from the front at a level of a few inches above the sidewalk. The foundation walls are built of brick and are about three feet thick. Flagstones, laid carefully, form the useful and lasting floor. The basement, as was the case in many houses of this period, was the center of the domestic activities of the household. Rooms for seamstresses, who worked under the supervision of the mistress of the house, play rooms for the children, storage rooms and rooms for the servants who were intimately connected with the family, were arranged here. Due to the good light and excellent ventilation this floor was ideally suited for its use.

The first floor is one full story above the ground, and is entered by a double flight of wide stone steps beginning at the street level on a slightly raised platform and meeting above on a broad stone landing. A wrought iron railing, simply designed, adds to the appearance of the façade. The front entrance itself is well designed and it is executed with a sympathetic feeling for detail and proportion, which characterizes the whole exterior of the house.

On ascending the front steps one is impressed with the feeling of privacy and security caused by the extreme height of the first or main floor above the sidewalk. It has been suggested that many houses in Charleston were built in this manner because the height of sea level prevented having a dry, excavated basement. There was no inexpensive and sure method of waterproofing at that time. However, in the case of the Gibbes House it is more reasonable to believe that the exterior design and the planning of the basement, so necessary to domestic life, were the governing motives in making the ceiling height of the ground floor so great.

It is evident that English-Georgian architecture influenced the character of the interior details. From the wide and impressive entrance hall on the first floor to the drawing room or ballroom on the second floor, the work is executed in the elegant manner of the designers who were popular in the mother country.

The first floor hall extends from the street entrance to the doorway from the garden approach—the entire length of the house. Unlike other hallways of the period, it is unbroken by an arch treatment. Columns and pilasters support the large span of the ceiling girder.

The stairway at the rear of the entrance hall is excellently proportioned. The graceful mahogany rail and the hand-wrought iron balusters add to the charm of the design. The stair landing forms a balcony across the full width of the rear of the hall from which a beautiful and unobstructed view can be had of the entrance and lower hall. The Palladian window on the landing gives a splendid view of the garden and thoroughly lights the lower and upper halls.

The fine proportions, the refinement of detail and the wonderful material are fitting monuments to the work of the master designer and craftsman. In fact, all the carved woodwork was brought from England. The carved ornament has a freshness and an originality that gives it character and individuality without overstepping the bounds of good taste. All paneling and woodwork is put together with care, showing that the work was done by cabinet-makers who took time to do things right and who spared no effort to get good results. All the wood wall panels seem to be in single pieces. The perfect state of preservation after over one hundred and fifty years of use is testimony as to the sincerity of construction and the lasting qualities of the materials. It is of interest to note that only the plaster of some of the rooms was injured by the earthquake of 1886, although the chimneys still show cracks. The house passed through the wars of 1775 and 1861 without injury.

The ballroom on the second floor is particularly interesting. The excellent proportions of this room are most pleasing. Two doorways, one opening into a withdrawing room and the other the entrance from the hall, are elegantly ornamented. The original and refreshing designs are all well executed. The ceiling with its Adam ornament is made of imported Italian stucco. This ceiling is the original. It has escaped injury and has never been changed or repaired in any way. Wood paneled walls, wide plank flooring in single pieces and a beautiful mantel complete this room. It would take hours of study to fully appreciate the proportions, the ornament and the execution of this wonderful design.

The second-story room adjoining the ballroom, which was probably once used as a withdrawing room and now as a bedroom, has been carefully measured for this chapter and the drawings are reproduced on pages 206–208. Pages 204 and 209 illustrate the unusual treatment of the pilasters on the chimney breast, the marble mantel and the cornice with its elaborate "drop" ornament.

One of the most interesting features of this fine old house is its garden, protected from prying eyes by a brick wall and well placed shrubbery. The desire for privacy seems to have been a governing motive in the design of many of the town houses of Charleston. Within this garden filled with plants of almost tropical vegetation, many of which are native to South Carolina, are found servants' quarters, a kitchen and storage space. The kitchen is equipped with a huge fireplace and a Dutch oven. Wide pine flooring—scrubbed white—gives the impression of cleanliness and domesticity associated with the colored servants of the Old South.

The Gibbes House and dependencies bear witness that the owner was not only a man of wealth, but also of culture and good taste.

This town house, inside and out, shows careful and intelligent study. Sometimes in our haste to praise all things foreign, we forget the great wealth of material we have at home. Our old houses are honest and sincere, inasmuch as they were designed and built to fill a local need. The Charleston houses are, it seems, particularly adaptable as an inspiration for the designing and building of the modern American home.

The Sloans have occupied and owned the Gibbes House since the Confederate War. Within the last few days, however, Mrs. Roebling, wife of the designer of the Brooklyn Bridge, bought the property. We can be assured that any repairs or restorations that are undertaken will be made sympathetically and that nothing will be changed which would in any way spoil this wonderful old landmark.

WILLIAM GIBBES HOUSE, 64 SOUTH BAY STREET, CHARLESTON, SOUTH CAROLINA

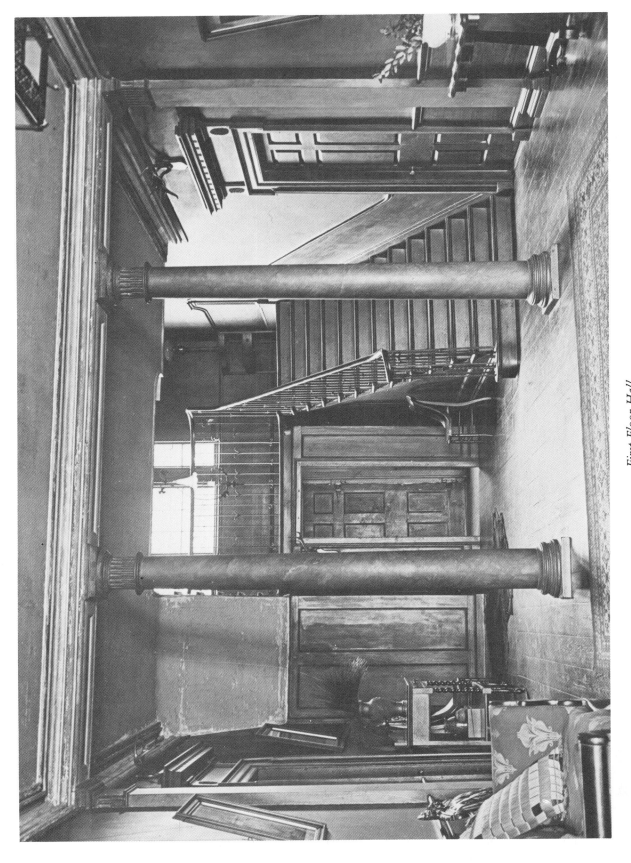

First Floor Hall

WILLIAM GIBBES HOUSE, CHARLESTON, SOUTH CAROLINA

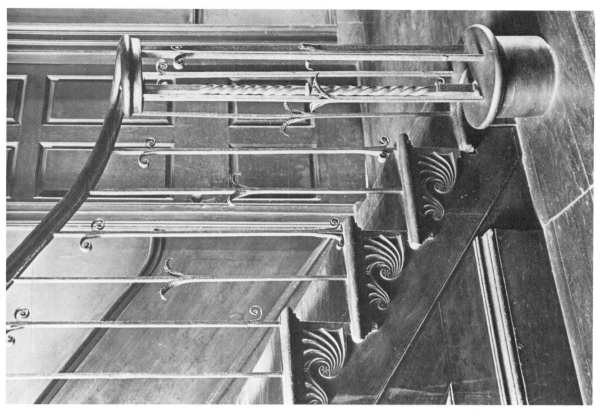

Newel and Stair Detail

Stair Detail
WILLIAM GIBBES HOUSE, CHARLESTON, SOUTH CAROLINA

Doorway and Stair, First Floor Hall
WILLIAM GIBBES HOUSE, CHARLESTON, SOUTH CAROLINA

Front Room, First Floor
WILLIAM GIBBES HOUSE, CHARLESTON, SOUTH CAROLINA

East Wall, Southwest Room, Second Floor
WILLIAM GIBBES HOUSE, CHARLESTON, SOUTH CAROLINA

Detail in Southwest Room, Second Floor
WILLIAM GIBBES HOUSE, CHARLESTON, SOUTH CAROLINA

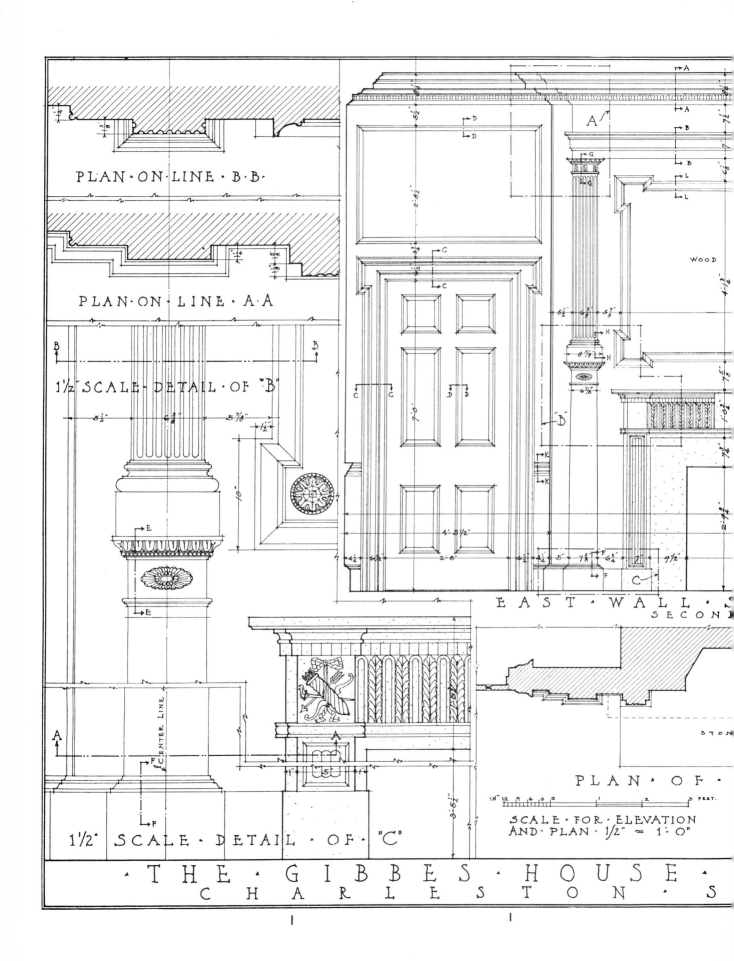

PLAN · ON · LINE · B · B ·

PLAN · ON · LINE · A · A

1½" SCALE · DETAIL · OF · "B"

1½" · SCALE · DETAIL · OF · "C"

· THE · GIBBES · HOUSE ·
· C H A R L E S T O N · S

E A S T · W A L L ·
SECON

PLAN · OF ·

SCALE · FOR · ELEVATION
AND · PLAN · 1/2" = 1'·0"

WOOD

STON

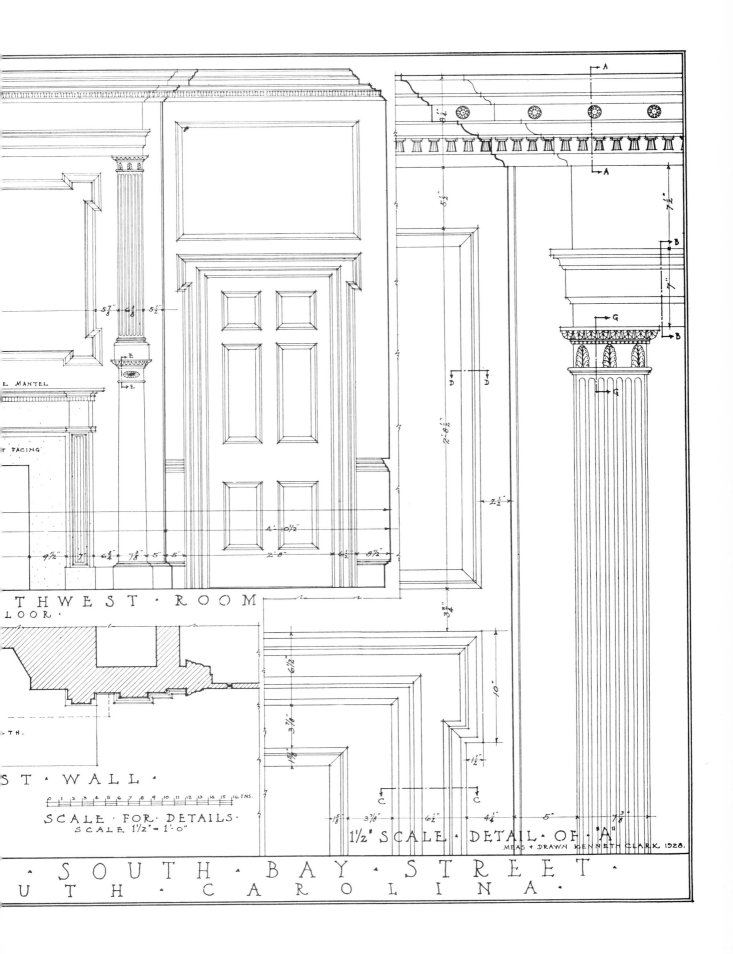

5⅞" · 6⅛" · 5½"

E

E

MANTEL

FACING

THWEST · ROOM
LOOR ·

9½" · 7" · 6¾" · 7⅞" · 5" · 5" · 2'-0" · 6½" · 8½"

4'-10½"

ST · WALL ·

TH.

0 1 2 3 4 5 6 7 8 9 10 11 12 13 14 15 16 INS.

SCALE · FOR · DETAILS ·
SCALE 1½" = 1'-0"

A

A

8¼"

5½"

2'-8½"

2½"

3¾"

6½"

3⅜"

1⅞"

10"

1½"

B

7½"

7"

B

G

D   D

G

C   C

1⅝" · 3⅜" · 6½" · 4¼" · 5" · 7⅜"

1½" · SCALE · DETAIL · OF · "A"

MEAS + DRAWN KENNETH CLARK 1928.

· SOUTH · BAY · STREET ·
UTH · CAROLINA ·

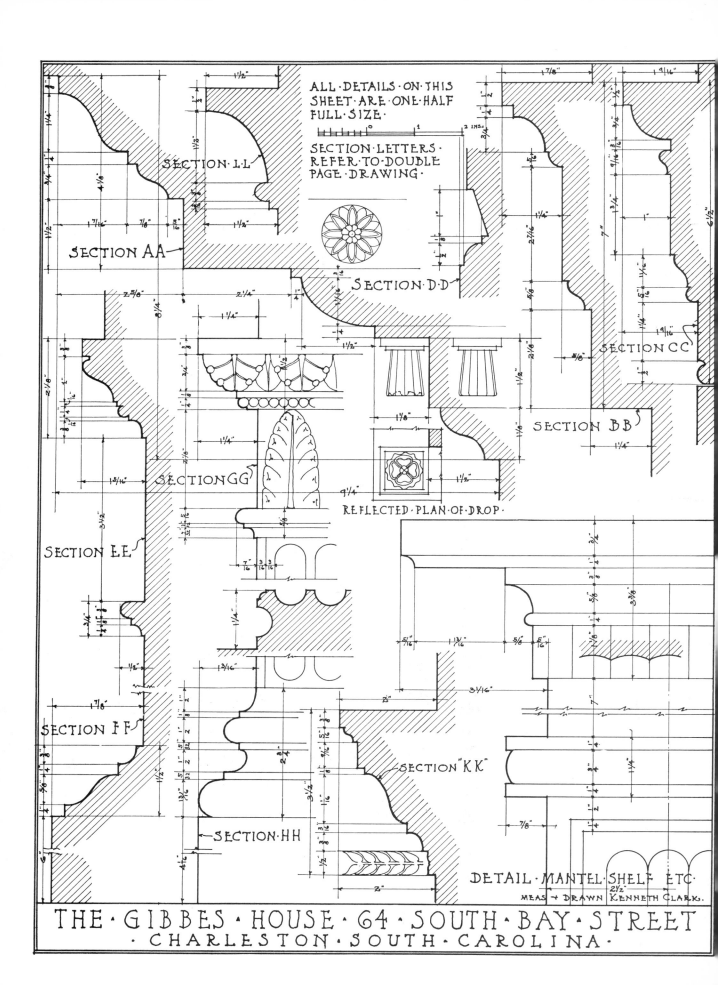

ALL · DETAILS · ON · THIS
SHEET · ARE · ONE · HALF
FULL · SIZE ·

SECTION · LETTERS ·
REFER · TO · DOUBLE
PAGE · DRAWING ·

SECTION · LL

SECTION · AA

SECTION · DD

SECTION · CC

SECTION · BB

SECTION · GG

SECTION · EE

REFLECTED · PLAN · OF · DROP

SECTION · FF

SECTION "KK"

SECTION · HH

DETAIL · MANTEL · SHELF · ETC ·
MEAS + DRAWN KENNETH CLARK ·

THE · GIBBES · HOUSE · 64 · SOUTH · BAY · STREET
· CHARLESTON · SOUTH · CAROLINA ·

Mantel Breast and Cornice Detail, Southwest Room, Second Floor
WILLIAM GIBBES HOUSE, CHARLESTON, SOUTH CAROLINA

Mantel in Ballroom
WILLIAM GIBBES HOUSE, CHARLESTON, SOUTH CAROLINA

Corner in Ballroom
WILLIAM GIBBES HOUSE, CHARLESTON, SOUTH CAROLINA

Detail of Ballroom North Door
WILLIAM GIBBES HOUSE, CHARLESTON, SOUTH CAROLINA

Detail of Ballroom West Door
WILLIAM GIBBES HOUSE, CHARLESTON, SOUTH CAROLINA

Ballroom, West Doorway, Second Floor
WILLIAM GIBBES HOUSE, CHARLESTON, SOUTH CAROLINA

Edwards-Smyth House, Charleston, South Carolina

Text by
Albert Simons
Photographs by
Kenneth Clark
Originally published in 1928 as White Pine Monograph
Volume XIV, Number 6

Detail of Entrance, 14 Legaré Street
EDWARDS-SMYTH HOUSE, CHARLESTON, SOUTH CAROLINA

THE EDWARDS-SMYTH HOUSE, CHARLESTON, SOUTH CAROLINA

IN a city of interesting buildings the Edwards-Smyth House is one of the most distinguished. While in every way the outgrowth of local, climatic and social requirements, it has moreover, that flavor of cosmopolitan sophistication that is ever an attribute of good breeding. While essentially a Charleston house, it could take its place without embarrassment in Blackheath, London, or in Lansdowne Place, Bath, where its later Georgian kinship would at once receive recognition. Designed for a subtropical climate where heat lingers and winter is only a pleasant interlude, it rises from a high arcaded basement above the spacious gardens and towers up three lofty stories to a roomy garret. No breeze can blow in from the harbor without entering one of its many tall windows, while the long piazzas shade the chambers from the ardors of the too intense sun of summer noons.

The servants' quarters are detached at a convenient distance from the house and bespeak a social order that provided gracious, if not always efficient, domestic service.

Thus far it is local and follows well established precedent. It is the thoroughly studied assurance displayed in combining all of the elements, the piazzas, the gates, the fence, the dependencies and the garden into a unified scheme that mark it as the work of more than the amateur. Many other houses in Charleston have employed all of these elements but none have combined them more happily. Let us consider the fence and gateway. If the house were not of such towering proportions it would be overbalanced by such monumental gates and posts, but the unity is sustained by using the same brickwork as in the house and preserving the same rather small scale throughout all of the detail. The gates combine the use of wood and wrought iron in a rather unusual but successful manner. The doorway, though simple, gains emphasis by being framed by two quadrants of wrought iron grilles and is approached by a short flight of marble steps curving outward in the most welcoming gesture. Within the door the steps continue up to the first story piazza.

The long many storied piazza is one of the most characteristic features of the houses of Charleston and gives the town much of its individuality. Seldom, however, do they tie in with the architectural composition and in most cases are frankly a compromise between correct design and convenience. In this case the matter has been handled with the greatest tact. A screen of brickwork has been carried across the street end which ties it to the house and serves as a setting for the doorway. This screen is finished by the cornice of the first story piazza. Looking through the fence we see repeated in two tiers the prolonged rhythm of eight widely spaced and very slender columns bearing very flat segmental arches. This type of arcade occurs frequently in Charleston and on one nearby plantation, but as far as the writer's observation goes, does not appear in quite this form in other American towns of this period, nor does there seem to be any English or continental precedent for its use. It is, however, obviously Adam in its inspiration and recalls those segmental vaults and arches that occur at Sion House and other Adam buildings which were in turn derived from vaults found at Pompeii, and in those charming stuccoed grottoes in the via Latina near Rome. These arch forms are not structural of course, but are only simulated in wood. However, the grace of line achieved, justifies this piece of architectural fiction. The capitals of the columns are typically Adam with a single row of slender laurel leaves about the neck. The banister rail is kept as simple and delicate in scale as possible in order that it may not interrupt the clean lines of the columns.

The brickwork of the house, while restrained, is worthy of note. The corners of the front are accented by long and short quoins of projecting brickwork and the stories are marked off in like manner by flat belt courses. In the flat arches over the windows, the bricks are ground so as to come to a straight line at the bottom and top and the mortar joint is kept to a uniform width. One other refinement has been introduced. As the Carolina "grey brick" is hand made and quite uneven along its edges, the joints have been filled with mortar of the color of the brick and then a narrow tooled joint has been worked in of white mortar. This narrow white line contrasts agreeably with the dull rust color of the brick.

Entering the stair hall from the middle of the piazza, we find that the plan of the building is quite simple, consisting of two large rooms on each floor separated by the hall. There is an addendum of smaller rooms at the back but this is obviously of later construction than the house and is of no special interest.

The stairway begins its flight on the left side of the hall and continues upward to the garret without a break in the continuity of the mahogany handrail. This rail is carried on delicate wooden spokes of rectangular section and stiffened at intervals by iron rods of the same appearance as the wooden spokes so that no newel posts are required. The hall ceiling has an ornamental plaster treatment consisting of a centerpiece of garlands of husks and radiating laurel leaves, and a flat band on the soffit of the stairs against the wall of a vine motif which is continued up through the second story hall. The rooms overlooking the street on both the first and second floors are given the more elaborate treatment, yet the back rooms are sufficiently ornate to make it quite evident that all four rooms were intended for the reception and entertainment of guests, the four rooms on the third and fourth stories being reserved for bedchambers. As the four main rooms are rather similar let us consider only the rear dining room on the first story and front drawing room on the second floor. In the dining room the rather chaste mantel of flat pilasters and garlanded frieze is set between two doors opening into closets formed by the chimney breasts. On the garden side between a door and a window we find an arched and paneled recess, the proper setting in which to enshrine the sideboard. Opposite the fireplace are two tall recessed windows overlooking the piazza. The architrave of all the windows comes just below the bottom plaster frieze and is enriched only with a band of simple reeding. The same architrave is carried around the door leading into the hall. All of the windows throughout the house have inside shutters that fold back into the jambs of the windows and show as panels on the face. There is a paneled wainscot about three feet high extending around the room. The band in the wainscot cap is enriched with swags indicated by short incised lines placed close together. Above the wainscot the plaster walls continue unbroken. There is a very flat plaster cornice at the ceiling with a plaster frieze below made interesting by an alternating rhythm of a group of channels and rosettes. (See illustration on page 234.) The general character of this room, though refined, is masculine and restrained,

it is the sanctum preeminently suited for the critical appreciation of Burgundy and Madeira. Here, nothing suggesting the frivolous has been tolerated.

In the second floor drawing room a much more ornate treatment has been carried out. The mantel has engaged columns of bold projection and the frieze has garlands and baskets of fruits and flowers, scrolls and attenuated rinceau while the mantel shelf curves outward in the center and inward at the ends. The hall door has not only an enriched architrave but a frieze and a cornice as well and is balanced symmetrically by a false door which if opened would plunge us down the stair well. The wainscot is similar to that in the dining room but it is in the plaster work that the greatest enrichment has been lavished. The centerpiece covers a considerable area of the ceiling and consists of six garlands of husks surrounding a circular band of alternating anthemion and palmettes about a huge rosette of wind blown acanthus leaves. The plaster cornice has a frieze bearing another variant of the anthemion motif while on the ceiling near the cornice are bands of countersunk reeding interrupted at regular intervals by enriched squares. The general effect of this room is much more gay and sumptuous than the dining room.

The bedrooms on the third floor have garlanded mantels, paneled wainscot, simple trim for doors and windows and very plain plaster cornices. The garret rooms are without fireplaces but are plastered and neatly trimmed, even on this story the windows have carefully fitted folding shutters in the window jambs. The workmanship throughout the house is uniform in general period and character.

Behind the house stands the kitchen with servants' quarters above and further to the rear is the stable and coach house with dormer rooms under the roof for the stable boys. These service buildings are separated from the garden by a screen of slender Tuscan columns with parapet walls between bearing panels of light wooden railings. Within the garden is a tiny octagonal tea-house with a pagoda-like roof. Rising in the midst of oleanders, spice bays, pomegranates and spikenards, it strikes an exotic note in harmony with the subtropical setting.

Documentary evidence as to the dates at which the property has changed title is available but in the lack of more specific information these dates are inconclusive in determining when the house now standing was built.

The property consists of two lots. The original grant was made to Richard Philips in 1694 and was later conveyed to Ralph Izard. In 1767 Ralph Izard conveyed to Barnwell Elliott. In 1784 the Master in Chancery conveys to Benj. Waller "all that certain brick residence and lot lately belonging to Ralph Izard." In 1816 George

Number 14 Legaré Street
EDWARDS-SMYTH HOUSE, CHARLESTON, SOUTH CAROLINA

Edwards bought a brick house and lot 52′ x 270′ for $20,000, and in 1818 the southern lot including a wooden house for $4,000.

The character of the house is most obviously post-Revolutionary as comparison with authentically dated Charleston houses will show. Owing to the very adverse economic conditions that prevailed in Charleston for

George Edwards that we owe the iron fence, gates and pillars as is evidenced by his intials G. E. in the grilles flanking the doorway and by the additional fact that he bought the southern lot making the complete fence possible. The fifty-two feet of the original lot ended at the south in the middle of the coach gate. In the house there is no evidence of remodeling or patching together

Mantel in Drawing Room, Second Floor
EDWARDS-SMYTH HOUSE, CHARLESTON, SOUTH CAROLINA

several years after the close of the Revolution, it is most unlikely that a building of this magnificence should have been erected between the evacuation of the town by the British in 1782, and 1784 when it passed to Benj. Waller. It is most improbable therefore, that the brick building on the property that came to Waller is the present dwelling. Now Waller owned the property for some thirty-two years from 1784 to 1816 and the writer is of the opinion that it was during this period in the revival of prosperity that this fine house was built. However, it is to

of work of different periods, so that the building of the house was carefully planned *de nouveau* and completed at one time while the same mode dominated. Even the gates, while later than the house, are much of the same period and suggest that they were built not many years later. While the above cannot be substantiated by documentary evidence it will doubtless satisfy most architects as plausible and the lack of specific dates will not deter their enjoyment of this very delightful building.

Drawing Room Doorway into the Second Floor Hall
EDWARDS-SMYTH HOUSE, CHARLESTON, SOUTH CAROLINA

Drawing Room Cornice, Second Floor

EDWARDS-SMYTH HOUSE, CHARLESTON, SOUTH CAROLINA

Dining Room Mantel
EDWARDS-SMYTH HOUSE, CHARLESTON, SOUTH CAROLINA

Drawing Room, First Floor
EDWARDS-SMYTH HOUSE, CHARLESTON, SOUTH CAROLINA

Entrance Gateway and Fence, Garden Side

EDWARDS-SMYTH HOUSE, 14 LEGARÉ STREET, CHARLESTON, SOUTH CAROLINA

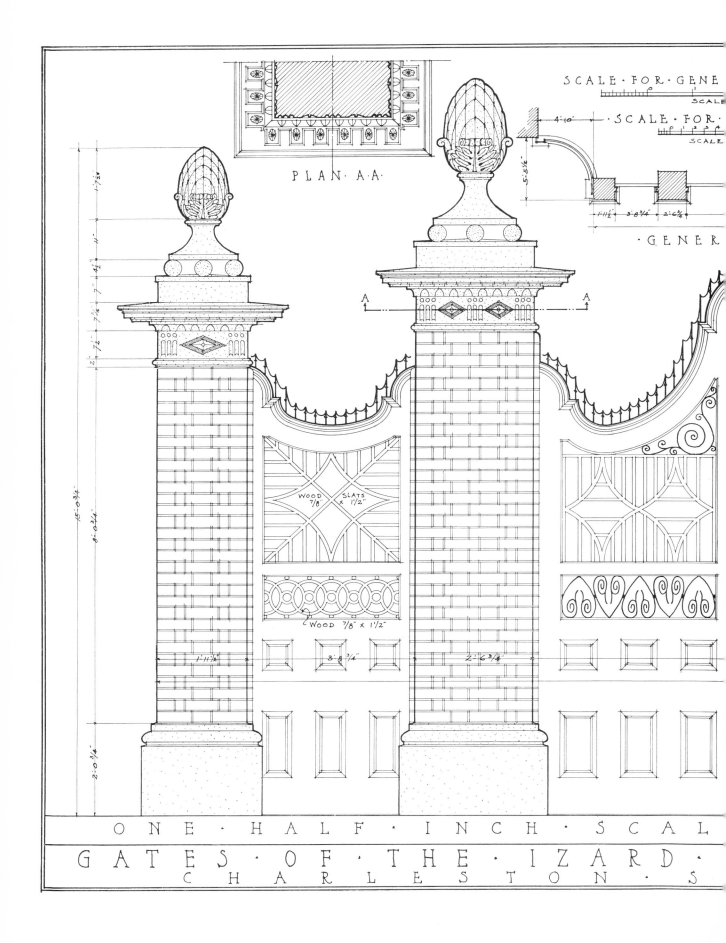

PLAN · A·A·

SCALE · FOR · GENE

SCALE · FOR ·

· GENER

WOOD SLATS
7/8" x 1 1/2"

WOOD 7/8" x 1 1/2"

O N E · H A L F · I N C H · S C A L

G A T E S · O F · T H E · I Z A R D ·

C H A R L E S T O N · S

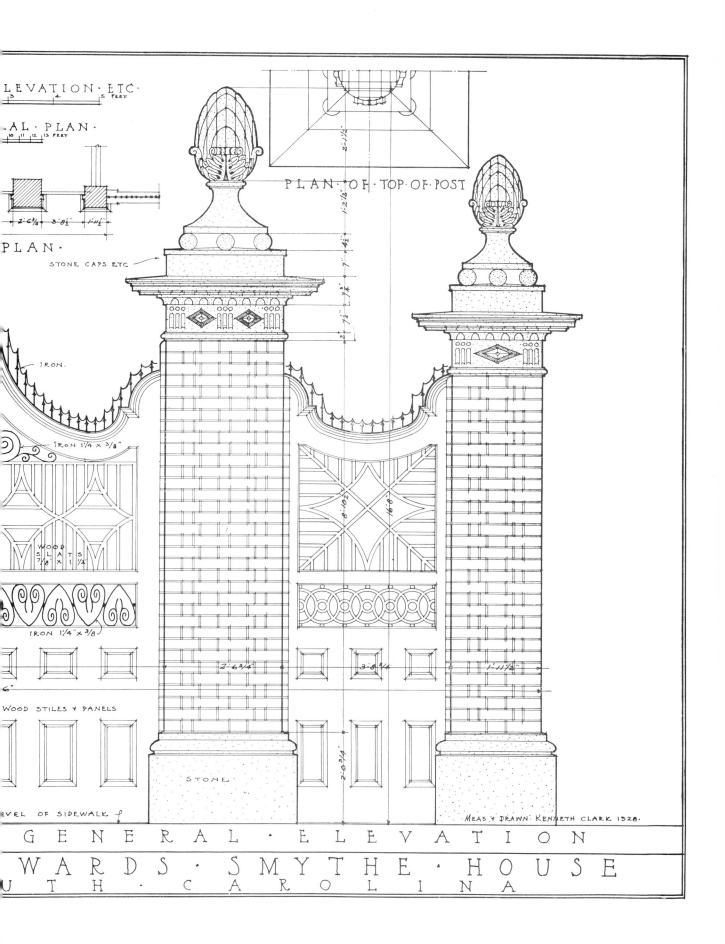

ELEVATION · ETC·
3   4   5 FEET

-AL · PLAN·
10 11 12 13 FEET

PLAN·

STONE CAPS ETC

IRON.

IRON 1/4 X 3/8"

WOOD
SLATS
7/8 X 1/2"

IRON 1/4" X 3/8"

WOOD STILES & PANELS

6"

EVEL OF SIDEWALK

PLAN · OF · TOP · OF · POST

STONE

MEAS & DRAWN KENNETH CLARK 1928.

2-6 3/4   3-8 3/4   1-11 1/2

2-0 3/4

G E N E R A L · E L E V A T I O N

WARDS · SMYTHE · HOUSE

UTH · CAROLINA

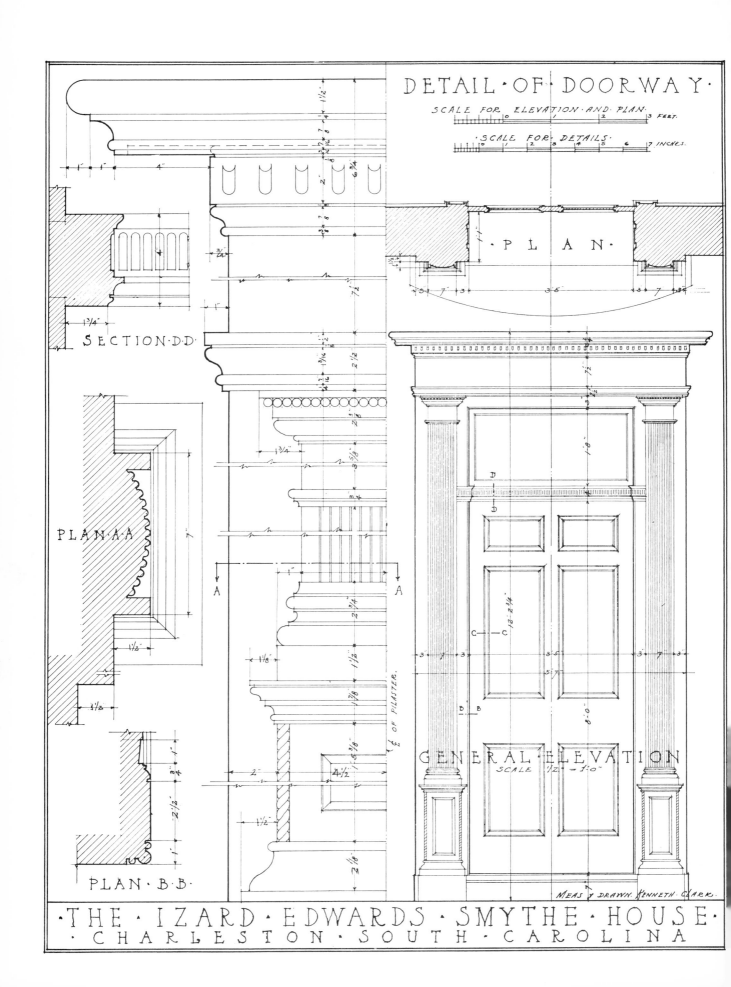

DETAIL·OF·DOORWAY·

SCALE FOR ELEVATION·AND·PLAN.

·SCALE FOR·DETAILS·

·PLAN·

SECTION·D·D·

PLAN·A·A·

PLAN·B·B·

GENERAL·ELEVATION
SCALE ½" = 1'-0"

MEAS & DRAWN. KENNETH CLARK.

·THE·IZARD·EDWARDS·SMYTHE·HOUSE·
·CHARLESTON·SOUTH·CAROLINA

Wrought Iron Grille Quadrant Framing the Entrance Doorway
EDWARDS-SMYTH HOUSE, CHARLESTON, SOUTH CAROLINA

Top of Gatepost
EDWARDS-SMYTH HOUSE, CHARLESTON, SOUTH CAROLINA

Gateposts and Fence
EDWARDS-SMYTH HOUSE, CHARLESTON, SOUTH CAROLINA

Servants' Quarters

EDWARDS-SMYTH HOUSE, CHARLESTON, SOUTH CAROLINA

Stable and Coach House
EDWARDS-SMYTH HOUSE, CHARLESTON, SOUTH CAROLINA

Detail of Dining Room Cornice
EDWARDS-SMYTH HOUSE, CHARLESTON, SOUTH CAROLINA

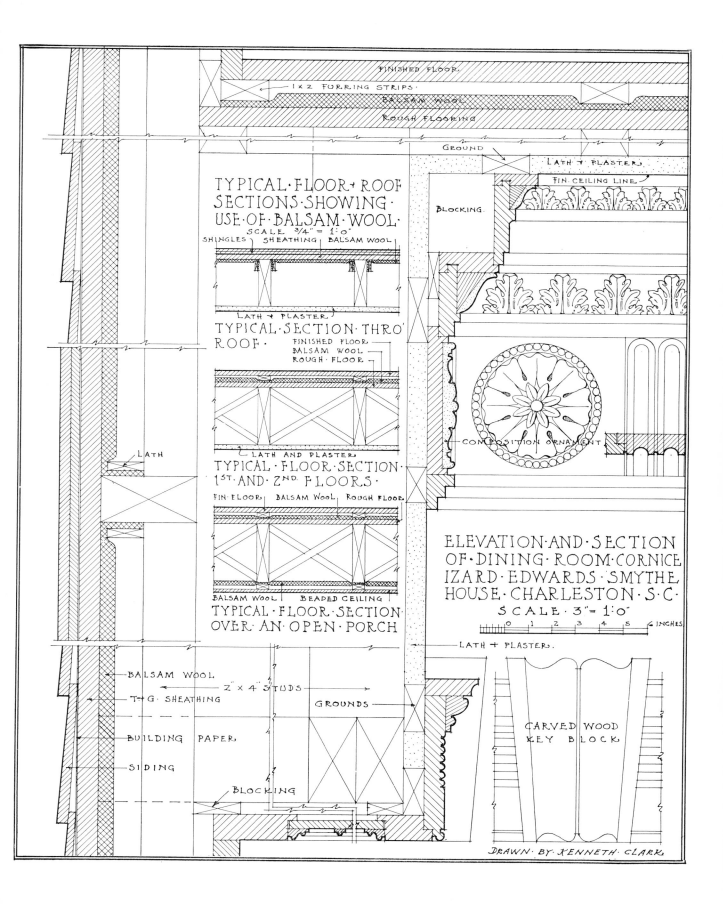

FINISHED FLOOR

1 x 2 FURRING STRIPS·

BALSAM WOOL·

ROUGH FLOORING

GROUND

LATH + PLASTER·

FIN·CEILING LINE·

BLOCKING·

TYPICAL·FLOOR·ROOF
SECTIONS·SHOWING·
USE·OF·BALSAM·WOOL·
SCALE ¾" = 1:0

SHINGLES   SHEATHING   BALSAM WOOL

LATH + PLASTER

TYPICAL·SECTION·THRO'
ROOF·

FINISHED FLOOR·
BALSAM WOOL·
ROUGH·FLOOR·

LATH AND PLASTER·

LATH

TYPICAL·FLOOR·SECTION·
1ST·AND·2ND·FLOORS·

FIN·FLOOR·   BALSAM WOOL·   ROUGH FLOOR·

COMPOSITION ORNAMENT·

BALSAM WOOL·   BEADED CEILING·

TYPICAL·FLOOR·SECTION·
OVER·AN·OPEN·PORCH

ELEVATION·AND·SECTION
OF·DINING·ROOM·CORNICE
IZARD·EDWARDS·SMYTHE
HOUSE·CHARLESTON·S·C·
SCALE·3"= 1:0

0 1 2 3 4 5 6 INCHES

LATH + PLASTER·

BALSAM WOOL·

T + G· SHEATHING·

2 x 4 STUDS·

GROUNDS·

BUILDING PAPER·

CARVED WOOD
KEY BLOCK

SIDING·

BLOCKING·

DRAWN·BY·KENNETH·CLARK·

End of Coach House and Fence
EDWARDS-SMYTH HOUSE, CHARLESTON, SOUTH CAROLINA